BIRMINGHAM SNOW HILL

A FIRST CLASS RETURN

DEREK HARRISON

PETER WATTS
Publishing

ISBN 0 906025 22 2

Published by
Peter Watts Publishing Limited
Gloucester

Design and layout: Derek Harrison/Peter Watts
Typesetting and artwork: Mopok Graphics, Glossop
Printing: Trio Graphics, Gloucester
Binding: Braithwaites, Birmingham

I have gone to great lengths to trace owners of photographs and acknowledge accordingly. My apologies to any source inadvertently overlooked, coupled with an assurance that any due acknowledgement brought to the publisher's attention will be readily given in any future edition.

(Front cover) Readers may care to note that the cover illustration is reproduced by kind permission of 'The Calvert Collection' from part of an original painting by Robert Calvert. Prints of the full scene, suitable for framing (size 27¼" x 17½") are available from: The Calvert Collection, 6 West Street, Tamworth, Staffordshire.

(Back cover) From an original Great Western publicity poster, loaned by Frank Burridge of the Big Four Railway Museum, Bournemouth.

A DEDICATION

In memory of my Mother and Father who encouraged me to record the history of Birmingham Snow Hill. To Leigh and Victoria — my children, who produced the basic idea for the covers.

A PERSONAL INTRODUCTION BY G. F. FIENNES, OBE

FORMER GENERAL MANAGER, BRITISH RAIL, WESTERN REGION

Snow Hill was always one of my favourite stations. For one thing Norrie, who became my wife, lived at Llangollen. Therefore whenever the 'King' or 'Castle' blasted away — I was going courting. Another thing, there had always been time, ample time, to get out and stretch my legs, inhaling the most peculiar air which that train shed permanently retained. The air was faintly baleful. It held a whiff of brimstone and was thick — almost palpable, as if a residue from a bygone age. It was easy to recollect the fulminations of Captain Mark Huish.

Mark Huish was, in the mid-nineteenth century, the General Manager of the London and North-Western. He thought that the Great Western, broad gauge and all, should remain bounded by a line running east and west through Oxford and Gloucester. All the territory north and west should be the province of the North-Western. He was a toughie, a railwayman after my own heart, whose aim and policy earned for the North-Western the title of 'Premier Line'.

If he had succeeded, there would have been no Snow Hill. Birmingham New Street would have become the hub of the railways of England over one hundred years earlier than it did. He very nearly did succeed. Having in his pocket already the line from Birmingham to Gloucester, he secured control of the projected line from Birmingham to Oxford. However, the House of Lords took a hand, and proceeded to justify W. S. Gilbert in 'Iolanthe'.

—'And while the House of Peers withholds
—Its legislative hand
—And noble statesmen do not itch
—To interfere in matters which
—They do not understand
—As bright will shine Great Britain's rays . . . .'

The Lord's legislated in favour of a duplicate line between London and Birmingham, namely that of the Great Western. Hence Snow Hill, in whose demise I took a small part a hundred and ten years later.

However, if Snow Hill had not existed, Derek Harrison could not have published a second volume of its history. That is something of a spin-off. He has been, and will be, a most versatile communicator by radio, lectures, and the written word, particularly on the subject of railways and not only in the Midlands. He was, for instance, seen recently at the new carriage depot at Crown Point, Norwich. In its early days this depot earned the title of 'The Bermuda Triangle' because trains went in and never came out. I gather Derek was not lost with all hands. That is good, because with his combination of an amateur's enthusiasm along with a professional's competence we would sadly have missed his second volume on Snow Hill.

Yours sincerely

Gerard Fiennes

Since this introduction was written, the author was saddened to receive the news of the sudden death of Gerard Fiennes in May 1985. He was all that was best in an English Gentleman — learned, considerate, witty, but above all — humane.

APERITIF

The original 'Salute to Snow Hill' appeared in March 1978. I little realised at the time that the history of this main-line station would captivate the public imagination.

The first edition was very well received by the reader and press alike. Much to my amazement this particular print was sold out within eight months! Therefore a reprint was put in hand.

So many ex-members of Snow Hill station staff, railwaymen and former travellers wrote to me, and not just from the Midlands. Enquiries were received from the United States and Canada, South Africa, — even as far away as Australia. Memories and photographs flooded in from persons who had known and loved the station in its hey-day. Therefore a new edition is not only a necessity — it is essential.

An interesting comment about Snow Hill came from one of its former Station Masters, who described the station as an 'establishment'. *"One had to be a very special person to work there also a very special person to use it."*

I did state in the first volume that I was *"mindful that the record remained incomplete"* but I feel a lot happier now with so much new information and photographs to present. However, the task of selecting suitable items for this volume has been monumental, although very rewarding.

Previous Station Masters' relatives have contributed such items as personal letters and photographs of members of the Royal Family taken in the 1920's through to the 1960's — without doubt treasure indeed.

A recent visit of mine to the Festiniog Railway recalls the numerous journeys undertaken from Snow Hill to Porthmadog by rail some twenty odd years ago. The fare then — ordinary second class return — was £2.7s.6d.!

Whilst chatting to Allan Garraway, the Festiniog's former General Manager, he mentioned that he had a small selection of photographs taken at Snow Hill in 1938 with an old VP camera. Later on during the evening he not only produced the photographs but the negatives also!

One is so grateful for all this material so carefully stored over the years yet, even as I write this now, there must still be that unusual photograph of Snow Hill lying undisturbed in an attic or drawer.

Here then is the result of all the painstaking efforts to bring this collection of pictures together for your enjoyment. I do hope you like it.

Derek A. C. Harrison
Barnt Green
Worcestershire 1985

CONTENTS

THE SNOW HILL STATION STORY

Snow Hill Station in Birmingham had many characteristics, the most significant being that it was not the meeting point of several railway companies — it was pure Great Western.

The Birmingham and Oxford Junction Railway — latterly absorbed by the Great Western — authorised the construction of a second rail route to Birmingham from London in 1846. This new line was built in Brunel's seven foot and a quarter inch gauge, or 'Broad Gauge' as it was then known.

The inaugural train from Paddington befell an unfortunate incident at a place called Aynho, near Banbury, when the express, filled with eminent Great Western Directors and their ladies, ran into the back of a local mixed train, causing some damage and considerable delay. Although no serious injury occurred to the passenger complement — only six complained of slight injury — it did demonstrate the enormous stability of Brunel's Broad Gauge.

Sadly, 'Lord of the Isles', the GWR's crack single-wheeler, could not continue the journey to Birmingham, due to a broken buffer beam. Therefore it was the somewhat less impressive locomotive of the mixed train that drew the passengers into Leamington for a belated banquet. Consequently the special never reached Birmingham on that significant opening day in October 1852.

The first station to occupy the site at Snow Hill, or the 'Birmingham Station' as it was then known, was a temporary wooden structure. However, as with most temporary structures in this country, it became permanent for nearly twenty years, lasting until 1871 when it was removed to Didcot for use as a carriage shed.

The Great Western realised at this time that the town of Birmingham — it did not achieve City status until 1889 — needed a more substantial station building.

This new station was a big improvement on previous accommodation. After a while, however, due to the smoky atmosphere that pervaded beneath the arched roof, conditions became somewhat stygian. Even the removal of glass from the end screens, along with several roof panels, did little to make matters comfortable for engine crews and passengers alike.

In 1854 a new line was opened, utilising mixed gauge tracks to enable broad gauge trains to work from Paddington through to Wolverhampton. By the mid-1860's the broad gauge was an encumbrance. Therefore on and from the 1st November 1868 all trains between London and Wolverhampton were being worked on the standard gauge of 4ft. 8 1/2ins.

As the years progressed towards the turn of the century it was painfully obvious that with increased rail traffic at Snow Hill the station needed expanding. As was stated at the time *"as fast as one train departs, there is yet another one waiting to squeeze into the station's narrow confines".*

In 1905, the Great Western Railway closed the hotel adjacent to the station with the exception of the dining room. Trade had steadily decreased over the years due to the fact that it was thought repugnant to stay anywhere near to the railway at that time.

With the decision taken to rebuild the station in its entirety the closing of the hotel became a godsend in as much as all the station staff could be accommodated in its commodious interior, thus allowing near normal rail operations to continue whilst reconstruction work started.

Walter Y. Armstrong, the GWR Works Engineer at this time, had many problems incidental to the site. Lateral expansion of the station was well nigh impossible due to the enormous expense of purchasing properties in the immediate vicinity. The Great Western Board questioned Armstrong very carefully . . . . *"what can we do to expand the station with the limited space available?"*

"Well, gentlemen, if we retain the former hotel as administration offices, then build the new station on three levels, cellars for storage of foodstuffs, the track bed level along with the station buildings surmounted by a glazed semi-open roof, coupled with this, extend the platforms in a northerly direction for some distance, I firmly believe we can accommodate the trains required."

Walter Armstrong won the day. During the period 1906-1912 Snow Hill was transformed into the most modern main-line station of its time and no expense was spared. The finest materials available were used to earn it the title 'The Great Western version of the Crystal Palace' — a fitting tribute to the nonchalant life-style of Edwardian England.

Happiness was, however, short-lived. Dark clouds were gathering over Europe and in August 1914 Great Britain declared war on Germany — a war which was to escalate world-wide. Troops, along with essential supplies, passed through Snow Hill. Many people at this time thought it all a 'great adventure'. *"It will all be over by Christmas"* was a commonplace cliché.

Peace did not return until 1918, by which time the road haulage business was becoming established, along with motor coach companies. Life would never be quite the same again.

The post-war period saw the advent of the cheap day rail excursion to places such as Stourport, Bewdley and Weston-super-Mare. On many a Saturday in the 'Twenties and 'Thirties any train after four o'clock in the afternoon to London attracted a return fare of 3s.6d. (17 1/2p). Last train from Paddington was at twelve midnight!

This carefree but economically depressing era carried on until the late 1930's when war with Nazi Germany became unavoidable.

Snow Hill could not slumber on through this grim reality. Evacuees were despatched into the country from its crowded platforms, for aerial bombardment was the new terrifying weapon of war.

The first bombs fell on the station in November 1940. It was in April 1941, however, that the more serious bomb damage occurred. Platform number five suffered the worst, but very little disruption to rail traffic ensued. Trains were running normally again within a matter of hours. One humorous event to appear from this misfortune was the pair of airman's trousers, along with a pair of lady's knickers, that remained fluttering in the girder-work for several weeks afterwards. As one would imagine many interesting stories abounded!

The return of peace again brought holidaymakers out in their thousands, all eager to escape the austerity slogans such as "IS YOUR JOURNEY REALLY NECESSARY?", along with "TRAVEL OFF-PEAK — DON'T CROWD OUT THE WAR WORKERS". With little or no petrol available for private motoring rail travel was the only means of getting to the seaside or into the country.

During the Second World War the railways were run to their very limits. Rail staff carried on with old and worn out equipment. Consequently, after the hostilities ceased, all four main-line companies turned to the newly-elected Socialist Government for help.

On the first day of January 1948, the railway system was nationalised, becoming British Railways. The spirit of the old Great Western, however, survived at Snow Hill. During the following period, passenger traffic increased to enormous proportions, the peak being reached in 1960.

In the late 1950's it was announced that the main line from Euston to Liverpool and Manchester via Birmingham (New Street) was to be electrified. An augmented hourly service from Wolverhampton (Low Level and Birmingham (Snow Hill) to London (Paddington) was inaugurated whilst the electrification work was carried out. Snow Hill's days were numbered. That last 'Golden Era' of steam on the Paddington line was truly glorious. 'Kings' and 'Castles' raced in their splendour through the Chilterns with such trains as 'The Inter City' and 'Cambrian Coast Express'.

Snow Hill station was limited in as much that it did not serve as wide an area of the United Kingdom as did New Street. If the tunnel became blocked at the south end then chaos ensued. New Street, however, has several entrances and exits and if a derailment occurred there, then trains could quickly be diverted into other platforms.

So, in 1967, the through service from Paddington to Birkenhead via Birmingham (Snow Hill) was withdrawn, Sunday 5th March being the last day that the station witnessed main line trains. 7029 'Clun Castle' earned the distinction of hauling the last steam-hauled train out of Snow Hill into railway history.

Decline had set in. Only local services now used the station, but these were gradually phased into either the rebuilt New Street or Moor Street stations until only the single unit railcar to Wolverhampton — via West Bromwich — remained.

In 1969 the former hotel was demolished, as it had become unsafe, along with the magnificent booking-hall concourse. All was reduced to rubble and steel scrap for the furnaces.

Saturday 4th March 1972 saw the very last train. By this time much of the station area was used as a car park. After this final departure the former pride of the old Great Western slumbered into decay, becoming a target for lead thieves along with dropouts seeking shelter on a cold winter's night.

It was five years hence, in 1977, that demolition began upon the main structure — a monumental task, for with limited clearances (Livery Street in particular presented problems), it had to be ensured that large areas of steelwork did not fall the wrong way. By the autumn of 1978 the station had been razed to platform level.

Good news! A new light will emerge from the tunnel once more. Plans have been drawn up to utilise the site again for rail transport.

Initially these plans, instituted by the West Midlands Passenger Transport Executive, consist of two island platforms, giving four track facilities. The actual station will be a terminal layout accommodating train services from the Shirley and Dorridge districts to the south of the Birmingham area. A further option to extend the line into Smethwick West, thereby linking up with the line to Stourbridge Junction, is catered for depending on the success of the first phase. Work has commenced on preparation of the track bed, along with new lighting in the tunnel, whilst the main station construction began during 1985.

1852-1905 VICTORIAN ADVENT

An early engraving of the Great Western Hotel as completed in 1867. Monmouth Street was later renamed Colmore Row. At the time this picture was published the temporary wooden structure of 1852 was still in use and not replaced until 1871 with a more substantial brick and steel station complex. In 1905 the hotel was closed for two reasons. The first was due to business falling away owing to the unsocial stigma of staying next door to a railway station. In Edwardian Britain this was considered repugnant. Secondly, the accommodation was ideal for conversion into railway offices for the Snow Hill station staff when the second rebuilding commenced in 1906.

(D. A. C. Harrison collection)

The official seal of The Birmingham and Oxford Junction Railway Company, which in 1846 authorised the construction of a railway line to Birmingham. It was latterly absorbed by the Great Western Railway.

(British Rail/Oxford Publishing Company)

An early photograph of the exterior of the Hotel, taken around 1900. Note, in the shadows of the nearby buildings, Hansom cabs in Livery Street and a cable car tram in Colmore Row. Also the heavy horse-drawn goods wagon headed by three horse power! This building was demolished during 1969 and 1970.

(D. A. C. Harrison collection)

Dean single wheeler 4-2-2 number 9 'Victoria' stands at the northern end of Snow Hill station — circa 1902. Without doubt this was one of the most handsome designs ever introduced on the old Great Western Railway, capable of a fair turn of speed. These single wheelers were used principally on the Paddington-Birmingham non-stop fliers, introduced in 1898. The end screens of the roof of the 1871 structure were glazed but quite early on in the station's life these screens were de-glazed to allow smoke and steam to dissipate from the rather gloomy interior.

(Real Photographs)

Snow Hill station about 1900 with 2-4-0 number 201 of the former West Midland Railway, originally built by Beyer, Peacock in 1862. These locomotives were entirely remodelled by the GWR at their Wolverhampton works, lasting in this condition until withdrawal in 1914. Number 201 is shown alongside Birmingham North Signal Box, its leading wheels resting upon the approach to Great Charles Street overbridge. This style of overbridge was built to an original design of I. K. Brunel. It is thought that Brunel had certain influences about the approaches to the north and south of Snow Hill station but no firm evidence is at hand to support this. The bridge girders were built with the unique round-topped style of platework to enable rainwater to drain off the parapets more easily.

(Leftwich & Co. Ltd)

517 class 0-4-2 tank locomotive number 566 simmers gently in the evening sunshine on the middle road of Snow Hill station circa 1904. The background depicts the 1871 structure. Judging by the general scruffy state of the buildings and some of the equipment, the decision to rebuild the station yet again by the Great Western Railway in 1905 came none too soon. Locomotive 566, however, lasted considerably longer than the 1871 station. It was constructed in December 1869 and after a hard service life working local passenger trains, coupled with pilot and occasional freight duties, was not finally sent to the scrapyard until May 1934.

(Real Photographs)

The 1871 Snow Hill station looking towards London — the arch of the main tunnel can just be discerned. Note the early Churchward 2-6-2 tank engine of the 39XX series on the centre road, the fashionable passengers standing on the wooden platforms, and the Victorian gas lanterns. With a rather gloomy interior a fair amount of illumination was necessary. A Refreshment Room was provided to cater for travellers — no details exist of its layout or the fayre available. This is the most detailed picture of the second Snow Hill structure to come to light — it is copied from an Edwardian postcard.

(D. A. C. Harrison collection)

The 1871 structure, as it was circa 1899 — a general view looking towards Paddington. The station pilot can just be seen awaiting its next call after shunting a local carriage set into the platform. Another set of suburban coaches stands in the bay platform to the right of the picture. Note also the various panels missing from the roof — a further precaution against the heavy sulphurous-laden atmosphere that permeated beneath the iron roof spans. The roof sections were manufactured and supplied by the Patent Shaft and Axeltree Company of Old Park Ironworks, Wednesbury. The early pattern gas lamps too, are of particular interest.

(D. A. C. Harrison collection)

Snow Hill 1904 — the thoroughfare from which the station eventually took its name, looking towards the main road intersection, Great Charles Street. Part of the original 1871 administration offices can be clearly seen on the left of the picture. The open-top tramcar is a delightful curio — these 'trams' were propelled by a continuous underground moving steel ropeway located in a cavity beneath the road surface. The engine house was situated at Hockley and now forms part of the WMPTE bus garage. During construction work of the Hockley flyover some of the cable support brackets were unearthed and donated to the Birmingham Science Museum and the National Tramway Museum, Crich, Derbyshire.

(City of Birmingham Reference Library)

Looking towards Wolverhampton in 1910 when the station was being rebuilt. Christopher Barron of E. C. & J. Keay designed the special erecting stage to enable the reconstruction to be carried on without interruption to rail traffic. As the work progressed the erecting stage was winched down the platforms until the commencement of the girderwork, which supported the booking hall concourse, was reached. The staging was then dismantled and returned to Keay's yard at Darlaston. The steam-operated winch hoisted up the steelwork before fixing and final rivetting into position. The carpenters and glaziers followed to affix the roofing materials. The station pilot, a GWR saddle tank of the period, shunts its way across the track complex. In this unique and rare photograph the original Great Charles Street bridge survives, to be replaced later by a much sturdier pattern. Also the platforms to the north of the station have yet to be constructed.

(E. C. & J. Keay/D. A. C. Harrison collection)

The first heavy girderwork to be placed in position during the Edwardian reconstruction was at the north end at a point near to Great Charles Street. This steelwork was to support the decking which carried the trackwork along with platform numbers 11 and 12. It is interesting to note the building aids in use in those days. These seem crude and cumbersome in comparison to the ultra-modern methods of construction in the 1980's. Note the rather primitive jacking and packing system used to manoeuvre each girder into the final position. Considering all this heavy reconstruction was carried out whilst trains were still operating, one can admire the tremendous amount of planning required to enable rail services to be maintained.

(E. C. & J. Keay/D. A. C. Harrison collection)

Looking towards Paddington circa 1911, with the final girders being moved into position for fixing before the new booking-hall concourse is constructed. The recently completed buildings and roof girders give the station an air of light and space. The famous clock on number 7 platform is fitted and working. Temporary wooden barriers were erected to prevent access to platform number 7, which is in the stages of completion. The paving slabs were manufactured by the Victoria Paving Company with a number of these treated with 'Victorite' carborundum to render them non-slippery. Note the early style weighing machine on the platform whilst some of the buildings on platform 5 have yet to be brought into use. The erecting stage is to be dismantled, its task now completed.

(E. C. & J. Keay/D. A. C. Harrison collection)

The south end of Snow Hill station in 1910 when the first of the supporting girders was raised into position in order that the new booking hall concourse could be completed. A GWR steam crane takes up the block whilst the slingers check that all is secure before the big lift. Note the bowler-hatted foremen and the straw boaters worn by the youth of the day. The flat cap was always the symbol of the workman around this period. The remains of the 1871 roofwork, somewhat decayed, awaits demolition in the background.

(E. C. & J. Keay/D. A. C. Harrison collection)

A general view of the girder complex at the south end circa 1910. The GWR 'Pollen-Trucks' were capable of carrying 60 tons of girders per pair from the James Bridge Works of E. C. & J. Keay Ltd. Each portion of girderwork was then hoisted into position before final rivetting. Railway officials look very much the executives of the day, complete with bowler hats and that eminently English characteristic — the umbrella. The staging for removal of the old roof covering and steelwork is in the mid-left of this photograph but the passengers have to be content with tarpaulin sheeting for protection until the new roof is erected.

(E. C. & J. Keay/D. A. C. Harrison collection)

The magnificent booking hall concourse as completed in 1912. The layout of the roadway was such that vehicular traffic entered through the right-hand side of splendid wrought-iron gates in order to set down passengers and luggage. Vehicles could then drive round the outer perimeter and out through the gateway to the left. Space in the centre was provided for vehicles requiring longer periods of stay but even this was limited in latter years. The walls were finished in imitation white Carrara Ware marble which gave a substantial amount of light and was easy to wash down and keep clean. Note the beautiful stained glass windows, also the two separate booking windows for excursion traffic.

(E. C. & J. Keay/D. A. C. Harrison collection)

Another view of the booking hall concourse, taken shortly after completion. What an age of elegance that period before the First World War must have been — the early motor-driven town carriages, the horse-drawn trap, and an early motor cycle combination add to this delightful cameo of life in Edwardian Birmingham.

The fashions of the time are equally interesting as passengers book their tickets; two schoolgirls gaze excitedly at a taxi cab, complete with steamer trunk, as it halts to allow the occupants to disembark.

(British Rail/Oxford Publishing Company)

The general layout at the north end after reconstruction work had been completed. A local train stands in bay platform number 9, being a stopping train from either Worcester or Bewdley via Kidderminster. A couple of six-wheeled suburban coaches stand on the line that led into the carriage sidings at Northwood Street. The photograph was taken using a large plate camera — the glass negative has, over the years, cracked but still produces a picture well worth keeping for its historic content.

(British Rail/Oxford Publishing Company)

An unusual view of Snow Hill, looking towards Paddington, taken after completion in 1912. The glazed windscreen, as originally designed and built, coupled with the Taylors' roof covering material, make an interesting comparison with photographs taken in latter years. The glass was removed from the central portion of the windscreen to enable smoke and steam to escape from the station interior. The roof covering the main portion was of the ridge and furrow type. A London-bound express, comprising of GWR clerestory coaches, stands in platform number 7 whilst passengers await the arrival of a train into platform number 5. The guardrail on the roof section of the main station complex served a dual purpose — that of a handrail and waterpipe. Brass tap connections were incorporated at intervals as a precaution against fire in the summer months; also to wash any industrial grime away from the glazing.

(British Rail/Oxford Publishing Company)

Snow Hill station boasted three booking offices. Besides those in the main concourse and Great Charles Street there was this smaller version on platform number 1 which served passengers' ticket requirements to stations on the Severn Valley line, Worcester and South Wales via Hereford, plus stations to Birkenhead. Note the station Foreman, impeccably dressed, even down to the Albert watch chain, and the equally immaculate passengers. Note also the GWR posters of the period, this scene being taken in 1912. The notices above each hatch read:

Great Western Railway
The issue of tickets at
this station will commence
20 MINUTES before the
departure of each train.

(British Rail/Oxford Publishing Company)

The sector table as installed, circa 1911. The idea behind this unusual but useful item of railway equipment, skilfully incorporated between bay platforms 3 and 4, enables a locomotive from an incoming train to be released in order to run round its train. It was supplied by Messrs Ransomes and Rapier of Ipswich. This operation was done by means of a portable release lever, which was slotted into the housing depicted in the mid-left of the photograph; the locking mechanism could only be freed when the signalman in the North signal cabin was satisfied that no danger ensued. He then released a lever on his own locking frame — thus on no account could the sector table be used without the signalman's knowledge. The bell in the upper part of the picture played a part in this operation. It was rung to inform the signalman on duty in the North box that the sector table was ready to be operated. Due to the high cost of maintenance the table was removed during the 1930's in favour of conventional run-round facilities.

(British Rail/Oxford Publishing Company)

Platform number 7 viewed from the bottom of the steps circa 1913, showing a typical London-bound express of the period. A variety of Great Western coaches are in the maroon livery in use at that time. Note also the ladies' fashions of this elegant era prior to the outbreak of the First World War.

(British Rail/Oxford Publishing Company)

ENTENTE CORDIALE!

Du Bousquet — De Glehn four-cylinder compound 4-4-2 Atlantic number 104 'Alliance' — named thus to commemorate the signing of the 'Entente Cordiale' — simmers gently at platform 7, circa 1913, before departing on a Paddington express. This particular locomotive was built by the Société Alsacienne des Constructions Mécaniques of Belfort, France in 1905, being similar in design to the Paris-Orleans '3001' class, which impressed G. J. Churchward, the GWR Chief Mechanical Engineer, to such a degree that he placed orders for number 102 'La France' in 1903 and numbers 103 'President' and 104 'Alliance' in 1905. This enabled the GWR to conduct a series of tests on the uses of compounding high and low pressure steam. Without doubt, all three locomotives proved extremely successful in traffic and were subsequently rebuilt by the GWR at Swindon. 'Alliance' ran for 778,830 miles before withdrawal for scrapping in September 1928.

(P. B. Whitehouse collection)

DINNER IS SERVED!

An impressive view of the Dining Room taken when the old Great
Western Railway Hotel building was still used for its original intended
purpose. The magnificent marble columns and oak ballustrade,
coupled with the beautiful stained glass screening, add to the
splendour of this period towards the outbreak of the First World War.
The elegant lace curtains, snow white table linen, and silver service
certainly made it the place to enjoy dinner whilst visiting
Birmingham. Woe betide any member of the dining room staff who
allowed a dirty mustard spoon to stray on to a table! Although the
Edwardian age was considerably elegant, only the monied classes
could enjoy its benefits. Work was not short but discipline was strict
and life could be rather difficult, with no state benefits in those days
if one lost a job.

(British Rail/Oxford Publishing Company)

RETURN FROM THE SOMME BATTLEFIELD

The booking hall concourse is illustrated, right, being now utilised for its wartime role of loading wounded soldiers from the many ambulance trains that called at Snow Hill from the south coast ports. A varied collection of ambulances warrants closer inspection. The vehicle to the left is certainly a Rolls-Royce Silver Ghost chassis fitted with an immaculate ambulance body. To the right is a Tilling-Stevens lorry fitted with a canvas tilt for protection against curious sightseers, not to mention inclement weather. When one investigates further into the various forms of transport of the 1914-18 period, it can be realised that Great Britain went to war in haste. We were ill-prepared weaponwise, and military road transport was very primitive, the horse still being a front line method of moving supplies. The railway was the only method of moving en-masse soldiers and equipment to the waiting ships that would convey Kitchener's 'Contemptible' little army to France. Due to the sudden need for extra trains, many holidaymakers were detained at the coastal resorts in order to prevent disruption of military traffic. After the initial declaration of war on 4th August 1914 the Birmingham Daily Mail printed the following passages . . . *"Busy scenes were witnessed at Snow Hill station during the morning. Reservists from all quarters of the city arrived with friends almost continuously . . . between nine and ten o'clock, two contingents of Territorials marched into the station, from their barracks . . . the total number on the platform by this time being about a hundred and twenty. All of the men expressed keeness to get to their duties . . . .''*

Throughout the war the British Government assumed control of the railways. The actual day to day control of rail transport was exercised through the Railway Executive Committee, comprised of General Managers from twelve of the more important railway companies, under the Chairmanship of the President of the Board of Trade. After the 9th August 1914 only troops were allowed on to the platforms of the main railway stations in Birmingham. In those early war days the men of the 'City Batallions' departed into history saying it would *"all be a joyride"* and would *"all be over by Christmas"*. Many Christmasses were to pass before it was all over. Meanwhile, local rail services diminished as more and more men were drafted into the forces.

It was not until 1920 that rail traffic workings were restored to pre-war standards. Acceleration of speeds was possible once the backlog of locomotive and track maintenance had been cleared. The First World War was indeed the end of an era. The conflict had changed men's minds and broadened their vision. The days of class privilege, along with the inequality, were numbered. Prior to 1914 railwaymen worked long hours, were poorly paid and subject to harsh discipline. In 1919 the stage was set for a showdown and a rail strike during that year lasted ten days, from 26th September until 5th October. It was long enough for men to buy surplus army lorries and set themselves up in the road haulage business. From this the gradual decline of the railway freight business began. Life somehow was never quite the same again.

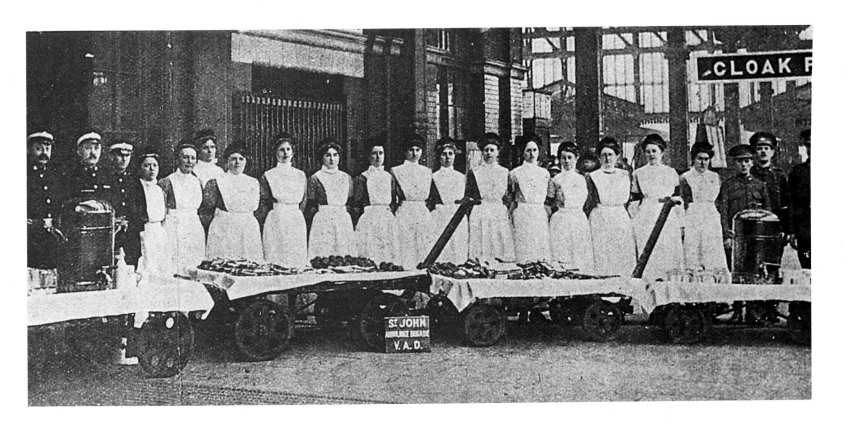

CHAR, WADS AND RE-ASSURANCE

Platform number 12 hosts a group of St. John's Ambulance men, along with a fine band of nurses, awaiting train loads of wounded soldiers from the battlefront. Note the luggage barrows temporarily used as makeshift tables to support two large tea urns and cups, along with bread and cakes, to give comfort to the war weary troops before they were transported off to hospital.

(D. A. C. Harrison collection)

'Star' class 4-6-0 number 4043 'Prince Henry' simmers gently at the northern end of bay platform number 4 circa 1923. The 'Stars' were originally introduced in 1907, followed by the 'Knights' in 1908. These new four-cylinder express engines were the very last word in locomotive design at that time and were to be seen on principal passenger workings from Paddington to the West of England, Birmingham (Snow Hill) and Wolverhampton for many years. In 1923 the first 'Castle' class locomotive left Swindon works. 4073 'Caerphilly Castle' was, more or less, an enlarged 'Star'. Several batches of 'Castles' were constructed between the years 1923 and 1950, whilst a number of 'Stars' were later rebuilt into 'Castles'. Note the rolling stock in the picture — certainly more modern although right up to the outbreak of the Second World War it was possible to travel on the Great Western main line in gas-lit wooden clerestory coaches built at the turn of the century!

(Photomatic)

Churchward-designed 4-4-0 'County' class number 3804 'County Dublin' stands at platform number 6 circa 1925, in all probability on a Hereford-bound express via Worcester. The 4-4-0 'Counties' were not very popular with engine crews as they had a tendency to oscillate violently due to the thirty inch piston stroke coupled with four large driving wheels working in concert. The rough riding was even more apparent whenever the locomotive was due for shopping at Swindon. All of the class had been withdrawn by the early 1930's.

(R. S. Carpenter collection)

The parcels yard at Snow Hill station in 1925. Note the extensive use of glazed bricks which gave off a tremendous amount of light where the area was restricted by roof obstructions. All parcels traffic in the Birmingham area was delivered by horse-drawn vehicles at this time — although a few motor-driven vans were starting to be seen on the streets of Birmingham. The horse and dray was to remain supreme until well after the close of World War II. The old style tapered milk churns were a commonplace feature at railway centres for many years and these were usually carried by rail in specially constructed vans known as 'syphons'.

(British Rail)

A 'Royal' visitor in the guise of the famous Great Western express passenger locomotive number 6000 'King George V', at platform number 6 on its first visit to Birmingham following the triumphant return from its 1927 visit to the Baltimore and Ohio Railroad Celebrations. The bell above the front buffer was presented to the locomotive by the B. & O. to commemorate the centenary of the company's founding. Also, as the locomotive was to actually run in the USA, it was an operating condition that the bell be fitted. This, of course, happened and 6000 still carries the bell to this day. Stationmaster F. A. Taylor is standing by the locomotive running plate.

(Nesta Taylor collection)

'Hall' Class 4-6-0 number 4928 'Gatacre Hall' awaits the right away with a Birkenhead express around 1930. Note the 3,000 gallon tender coupled to the clerestory-roofed coaches, dating from the turn of the century. Another interesting feature of the 'Hall' class locomotives around this period was the lamp iron in front of the chimney. Eventually all were removed to the front of the smokebox door, the last being converted in this way by 1939.

(Real Photographs)

PERIOD SETTING

6011 'King James I' pauses in the up middle road at Snow Hill before proceeding to its next spell of duty. Not an actual photographed event but a very well-executed painting by Wilfred Brewhill. Many paintings of Snow Hill station have appeared over the years — this is a rather unusual view depicting the mid-1930's era. One can almost smell the smoke, the warm oil, and feel the heat from the burning coal.

(L. C. Jacks collection)

DIESEL DEBUT — THIRTIES STYLE

Unusual visitor to Snow Hill on Sunday 24th April 1932 was a specially designed and equipped railcar known as the 'Micheline', loaned from France in order that various English railway companies at that time could collate information regarding the use of rubber tyres fitted to the sides of the rail wheels, which enabled silent running. Michelin Tyres sponsored the experiment. The railcar is pictured on that Sunday as the centrepiece of what appears to be a first-aid exercise — obviously attracting much interest from railwaymen and passengers alike. The odd-looking cylindrical containers on each side of the front cab are, in fact, exhaust coolers for use when the railcar ran in the reverse direction. No order for these vehicles was ever placed by the Great Western, although some of the findings must have been noted as the first AEC-built railcars were introduced by the GWR in 1934.

(Geoffrey Hughes collection)

"Whisky and soda, Sir?" The smartly-dressed conductor/steward serves drinks to passengers en-route to Cardiff during a pre-service run from Snow Hill for members of the press in July 1934. The interior of the diesel railcar was very well appointed with a table at each set of four seats, with seating and curtain materials supplied by Messrs. Heales of London. Without a doubt the last word in high speed luxury at that time. The diesel cars were capable of over 70 mph and gave many years service before withdrawal in the early 1960's.

(British Rail/Oxford Publishing Company)

Streamlined diesel railcar number 4 enters platform 8 and will continue on down to halt at number 7 platform before taking on passengers for Newport and Cardiff via the North Warwickshire line, Stratford-upon-Avon and Cheltenham Spa (Malvern Road). This unique service was introduced in July 1934 by the GWR as an economy measure when the running of a through express to Cardiff proved uneconomical. The railcar carried 44 third class only passengers with full toilet and refreshment bar facilities. An extra 2/6d (12½p) supplement was charged in addition to the normal third class single fare and the service proved extremely popular. The railcar depicted is now preserved and can be seen at the Great Western Railway Museum, Swindon.

(Allan Garraway, MBE)

BIRMINGHAM (SNOW HILL) — CARDIFF DIESEL SERVICE.
JULY 1934.

KING OF THE ROAD!

6013 'King Henry VIII' at the end of number 12 platform in 1935 on a Paddington-bound express. An unusual viewpoint this as most London trains departed from platform number 7. Of note is the heavy girderwork supporting the sloping walkways that led down from the main booking hall concourse. The Black Country engineering firm of E. C. & J. Keay Limited of Darlaston, whose company emblem was that of a Staffordshire knot, supplied almost 6,500 tons of wrought iron and steel for the 1906-1912 reconstruction of Snow Hill station. It was in 1927 that the famous 'King' class appeared, born initially for prestige purposes as the Southern Railway up to that year possessed the most powerful passenger 4-6-0 in the country. Sir Felix Pole, the erstwhile General Manager of the Great Western decided to build an even larger, more powerful locomotive. The Great Western was considered the finest in the world at that time. Therefore it was an all out drive to captivate the public's attention — *'Might and Majesty'*, *'The King of Railway Locomotives'*, and so on. The main drawback with the new class was the weight restriction — the axle loading was 22½ tons! — thereby confining them to double-red express routes, such as Paddington to Plymouth, Paddington to Birmingham (Snow Hill)/ Wolverhampton, and latterly Paddington Cardiff via the Severn Tunnel. In 1935, Great Western Centenary Year, number 6014 'King Henry VII' was turned out with a rounded 'bullet-nose' along with semi-streamlined cowlings — not exactly a success but a feeble attempt at countermanding wind resistance. The Great Western never went in for streamlining as such and the locomotive quickly returned to the normal outline, although the wedge-shaped cab remained a feature of 6014 until final withdrawal from Wolverhampton (Stafford Road) shed in September 1962. Thirty 'Kings' were built at Swindon works between June 1927 and August 1930. Three now survive — number 6000 'King George V' at Bulmers Railway Centre, Hereford; 6024 'King Edward I' at Quainton Road, Buckinghamshire; and the third, 6023 'King Edward II' has been purchased for £21,000 by Harvey's of Bristol. After restoration at Bristol Temple Meads station, number 6023 will be used for steam-hauled excursions based on Bristol — the city it served for so many decades.

(Frank Hemming)

HOME WITH THE MILK!

The Bulldog Breed — 4-4-0 'Bulldog' class number 3442 'Bullfinch' enters Snow Hill station with an up milk train in the summer of 1937. Note the gas tank wagon to the right. These tanks were used at country stations not usually connected to a mains gas supply. Northwood Street sidings was specially equipped to recharge wagons of this nature. It was then a matter for the charged vehicle to be attached to a passenger or freight train for delivery to the appropriate destination.

(L. Hanson)

Taken from the North signal box is this general view of the crossing lines and scissor-like pointwork of Snow Hill North. An unidentified 'Star' class 4-6-0 pulls out of platform 6 towards Wolverhampton whilst a 2-6-2 prairie tank shunts rolling stock into number 11 platform on the left. The splendid smoke effect from the departing express adds to this superb railway scene from the mid-1930's.

(Birmingham Post and Mail)

A

B

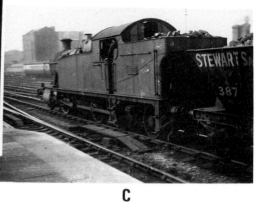

C

PRE-WAR SNOW HILL SNAPSHOTS — Allan Garraway MBE

Scenes from an enthusiast's photo album. The following six photographs were taken by a youthful Allan Garraway in 1938. He was visiting Stourbridge to spend a holiday with a school chum; a day at Snow Hill was a 'must' in the programme of events.

D

F

E

A. Large 2-6-2 prairie tank number 8101 and an unidentified 'Bulldog' 4-4-0 pause from their labours at the north end of Snow Hill. The 'Bulldog' is in all probability on station pilot duties. 8101 will be on its way to Tyseley shed for servicing before working a local service in the Birmingham area.

B. This picture shows a comprehensive auto-train of three coaches with an erstwhile GWR pannier tank in the centre. These auto-trains were a common sight on the GWR, used mainly for branch line and local services. The unique feature about them was the fact that they could be driven from the vestibule located at the end of the specially-equipped 'autocoach'. The fireman remained on the locomotive and by a series of rods and couplings the driver controlled the speed. There was also a vacuum brake lever in the vestibule.

C. Swindon-built heavy duty 2-8-2 tank locomotive number 7256 drifts through in the Wolverhampton direction with a heavy iron ore train. These sturdy tank engines were designed for hauling heavy freight trains — particularly coal traffic from South Wales — to various parts of the Great Western system. Note the Stewarts and Lloyds name on hopper wagon number 387, denoting private ownership.

D. 2916 'Saint Benedict' about to depart from bay platform number 3 with a semi-fast train to Worcester, Malvern and Hereford. Note the somewhat sparse protection offered to the crew due to the small cab roof. Without a storm sheet, which was not always fitted for inclement weather, the cab of a 'Saint' could be a most unpleasant place to be when working tender first!

E. An unidentified 'King' dashes into Snow Hill from the Wolverhampton direction with an up Paddington express. Although this picture is a little blurred, it shows the 'King' as originally built with a single chimney. Whenever and wherever these majestic locomotives put in an appearance it was guaranteed to turn a head or two.

F. An unnamed 'Bulldog' 4-4-0 enters Snow Hill with an up semi-fast to Leamington Spa. Considering the limited potential, with a single-speed vest pocket camera, Allan did extremely well to capture some interesting railway scenes at Snow Hill in this uneasy period before the outbreak of World War II.

G.W.R. PROPOSED. NEW HOTEL. SNOW HILL. BIRMINGHAM

WHAT MIGHT HAVE BEEN

In April 1939 the GWR announced that it was to build a new modern hotel adjoining Snow Hill station, on the site of the original hotel of the 1860's. It would have had frontages in Livery Street, Colmore Row and Snow Hill, with six floors and a steel-framed backbone. A natural Portland Stone facing similar to the Great Western Railway Headquarters at Paddington would have greatly enhanced this rather dull side of Birmingham. The ground floor was designed to house reception offices, hall, lounge, cocktail bar and cloakrooms. On the first floor a dining room for 150 people, a spacious lounge and smoke room, plus three private meeting rooms which could be converted into a banqueting suite for 160 plus, were planned along with display stock rooms, space for trade shows and kitchen accommodation for all the hotel area. The remaining five floors would have contained 28 double rooms, 142 single rooms (all with private bathrooms); also a private suite on each floor. Full central heating and air conditioning with a comprehensive fire door system affording safety and comfort to all patrons was planned. The main entrance would have been in Colmore Row with direct access to the main Booking Hall concourse. Work should have commenced in the autumn of 1939 but due to the outbreak of war the plans were shelved and not proceeded with on cessation of hostilities.

(British Rail)

BUSINESS AS USUAL!

Platform number 7 in the autumn of 1939. The telegraph office is heavily sandbagged in anticipation of widespread bombing on the outbreak of war on 3rd September. The bombing did not take place until the November of 1940 but the railway executive were taking no chances. The telegraph office was an important communications centre — by sandbagging the walls and windows this did offer a good form of protection against flying glass and splinters. The two photographs show that it is business as usual and no amount of threats from Nazi Germany will deter the Great Western Railway from carrying out its duties in serving the telling public. Another interesting feature is the collection of pigeon baskets returning to their home station via Snow Hill. Pigeon racing is a very popular sport in the Midlands and most main line and suburban stations catered for the needs of the bird fanciers — the GWR even ran pigeon specials from time to time.

(British Rail/Oxford Publishing Company)

READY TO SERVE!

A wartime photograph of the Snow Hill emergency fire brigade, taken circa 1941, showing the men turned out in oilskins and waterproofs with the inevitable tin hat. The Snow Hill Station Master, Arthur Hammond Elsden, stands to the right of the picture.

(Birmingham Post and Mail/Mrs D. Tipping collection)

The ladies of Snow Hill, not to be outdone, and rightly so, also displayed their courage and tenacity in dealing with any emergencies resulting from an incendiary attack. The porteresses and telegraphists are pictured standing in front of the Berisford auxiliary fire pump which was the standard issue to all fire services nationwide at the time.

(Birmingham Post and Mail/Mrs D. Tipping collection)

SALVAGE FOR VICTORY!

A display of reclaimed materials exhibited in a former LMS dining car during August 1944. The exhibition utilised materials salvaged from various resources that would normally have gone to the incinerators and now were put to new uses in all aspects of winning the Second World War. The aircraft depicted in the background is a Short Sterling — many of the salvaged materials on display were used by the aircraft industry at this crucial point of the war. The GWR, in fact, reclaimed 250,000 tons of scrap metal in addition to tens of thousands of tons of waste paper, worn out harness, old bones, rope, string and obsolete machinery. Even the letters forming part of the title theme 'Found in every British home' are the old cast-iron nameboard letters removed from platforms upon the direct order of the Government as an anti-invasion measure. Station Master A. H. Elsden presides over the proceedings.

(Birmingham Evening Despatch/Mrs D. Tipping collection)

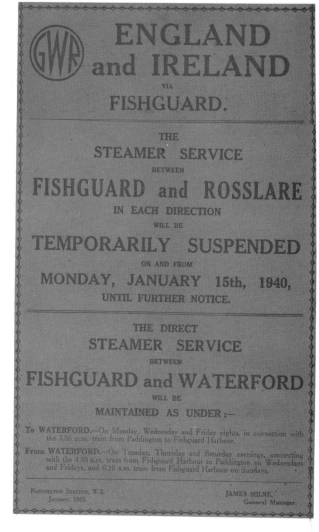

GWR

ENGLAND and IRELAND
VIA
FISHGUARD.

THE
STEAMER SERVICE
BETWEEN
FISHGUARD and ROSSLARE
IN EACH DIRECTION
WILL BE
TEMPORARILY SUSPENDED
ON AND FROM
MONDAY, JANUARY 15th, 1940,
UNTIL FURTHER NOTICE.

THE DIRECT
STEAMER SERVICE
BETWEEN
FISHGUARD and WATERFORD
WILL BE
MAINTAINED AS UNDER :—

To WATERFORD.—On Monday, Wednesday and Friday nights, in connection with the 7.55 p.m. train from Paddington to Fishguard Harbour.

From WATERFORD.—On Tuesday, Thursday and Saturday evenings, connecting with the 4.35 a.m. train from Fishguard Harbour to Paddington on Wednesdays and Fridays, and 6.10 a.m. train from Fishguard Harbour on Sundays.

PADDINGTON STATION, W.2.
January, 1940.

JAMES MILNE,
General Manager.

BEFORE AND AFTER

Two wartime views of platform number 5. The first, taken the morning after an air attack in April 1941, shows the bookstall, along with the Ladies Waiting Room, entirely destroyed. The second picture displays a transformed scene with the rubble cleared away and a new concrete support pillar in situ ready to receive new cast-iron coverings. A gaping hole still remains in the roof but considering the saturation density of the wartime bombing on Birmingham, Snow Hill station came off lightly. After the cessation of hostilities a reglazing of the entire station roof and side-screens was undertaken, beginning in 1946.

(British Rail)

Air-raid damage, 9th-10th April 1941, after a night of heavy bombing in Birmingham. Snow Hill suffered damage to various parts of the station complex but one piece of good fortune that befell the station was that in spite of major damage, traffic was not disrupted for very long. In these two rare photographs one of the bombs had penetrated the steel decking close to platform number 11 and carried on down into the parcels yard, where brickwork has been dislodged and windows blown in. Fortunately the trackwork alongside platforms 11 and 12 remained intact and after an initial inspection was passed as fit for traffic. The wooden telescopic tower in the background of the right-hand photograph was used for gaining access to the lighting system throughout the station, as many of the sockets and lampholders were situated high up in the roofing complex.

(Both British Rail, courtesy Public Records Office)

GREAT
WESTERN
RAILWAY
GOODS
AND
PARCELS
RECEIVING
OFFICE

'King' class 4-6-0 number 6001 'King Edward VII' at Snow Hill on a Paddington-Wolverhampton train in May 1945 — one could hardly call them expresses in those days as 60 mph was the maximum speed permissible due to wartime conditions. The side windows of the cabs have been removed and blanked out to enable the anti-glare weather-proofed 'tent' to be installed. These fully enclosed tarpaulin bags were fitted to prevent the glare from the firebox being detected by enemy aircraft. As one could imagine, working on a fully enclosed footplate with the heat from the firebox all around bore resemblance to a mobile Turkish bath. As the air attacks receded, the 'tents' were removed, along with the blanking plates, to enable the side windows to be reinstated.

(E. E. Smith)

GREAT WESTERN RAILWAY.
Emergency Passenger Train Service from Birmingham (Snow Hill).

These Services are liable to alteration or cancellation at short notice.   For details see Company's Time Tables and Notices.

TO	WEEK-DAYS.	SUNDAYS.
LONDON (Paddington)	7к30, 9к0, 10.58 a.m., 12к0 noon, 3к0, 4к0, 6к0, 7.55 p.m., 12.25 night.	11к40 a.m., 6.35, 8.2z p.m.
WARWICK and LEAMINGTON SPA	5.20, 6.22, 7.30, 8.0, 9к0, 9.6, 10к58, 11.5 a.m., 12к0 noon, 12к25, 12.47, 1.20, 2.5, 3к0, 3.10, 4.0, 4к53, 5.20, 6к0, 6.3, 6.45, 7.20, 7.55, 8.20, 9.40, 11.5 p.m., 12к25 a.m.	9.0, 10.28, 11к40 a.m., 12.25, 3.35, 5.25, 6.35, 8к22, 8.40, 9.50 p.m.
BANBURY, OXFORD and READING	5с20, 7к30, also 9к0 a.m., 10.58 a.m., 12к0 noon, 1.20, 3к0, 4к0, 6сх0, 7.55 p.m., 12.25 night.	10.28, 5.25, 6к35, 8.22 p.m.
CHELTENHAM SPA GLOUCESTER, NEWPORT, CARDIFF and SOUTH WALES	9.10 a.m.	See L.M.S. Co.'s Time Table.
BRISTOL & WEST OF ENGLAND (via Hereford)	7†30, 10.30 a.m., 1.0, 3.50. 5v0, 7†v55, 8.20 p.m. (Birmingham and Bristol Direct Services temporarily suspended. (See L.M.S. Co.'s Time Table).	12.0 noon, 5.10 p.m.
SOUTHAMPTON, PORTSMOUTH & SOUTHSEA & BOURNEMOUTH	7.30, 10к58 a.m., 12к0, 1.20, 4.0, 7.55, 12.25 night.	10.28 a.m., 5.25 p.m.
STRATFORD-ON-AVON	6.22, 7.32, 9.10, 11.5 a.m., 12к25, 2.5, 4.0, 5.55, 6.35, 6.45, 7.20, 9.40, 10к50 p.m.	9.5 a.m., 12.25, 12.40, 3.40, 6.0, 7.10 p.m.
OLTON, SOLIHULL and KNOWLE and DORRIDGE	5.20, 6.22, 7.4, 7к18, 7х30, 7.39, 8.0, 8.32, 9.6, 11.5, 11.45 a.m., 12.10, 12m25, 12s40, 12.47, 12к55, 1к810, 1.20, 2.5, 3.10, 4.20, 4к640, 4сm53, 5с10, 5.20, 5оm45, 5бк47, 6.3, 6.12, 6m35, 6.45, 7.20, 7о40, 8.20, 9.40, 10.40, 11.5 p.m.	10.28 a.m., 12.25, 12.45, 3.35, 5.25, 6.0, 6х35, 8.40, 9.50 p.m.
SHREWSBURY, CHESTER, BIRKENHEAD and LIVERPOOL	4.10, 6.0, 8.20, 8.33, 11к46 a.m., 1к38, 4к45, 6кn41, 8к50 p.m.	4.21, 7к0 a.m., 1.40, 2.45, 8кn46 p.m.

For Notes see page 495.   Continued on page 494.

GREAT WESTERN RAILWAY.
Emergency Passenger Train Service from Birmingham (Snow Hill).

These Services are liable to alteration or cancellation at short notice.   For details see Company's Time Tables and Notices.

TO	WEEK-DAYS.	SUNDAYS.
WOLVERHAMPTON (Low Level)	4.10, 5.30, 6.0, 6.30, 7.40, 8.20, 8.33, 8.45, 9.26, 10.10, 11.17, 11к25, 11.45, 11к58 a.m., 12s30, 12s45, 1.15, 1.38, 2.7, 3.0, 4.5, 4.45, 5.10, 5.30, 5.40, 5.55, 6.18, 6.41, 6.45, 7.14, 7.50, 8.15, 8.50, 10.0, 11.5 p.m.	4.21, 7.0, 10.30 a.m., 12.50, 1.40, 2.45, 6.10, 7.42, 8.46, 9.30, 10.25, 11.32 p.m.
CREWE and MANCHESTER	6.0, 10.10 a.m., 4.45, 8.50 p.m.	7.0 a.m., 8.46 p.m.
ABERYSTWYTH and CAMBRIAN LINE	6.0, 8.33 a.m., 1.38 p.m.	4†21 a.m.
HANDSWORTH and SMETHWICK	5.30, 5.40, 6.15, 6.30, 6.45, 7.17, 7.37, 7.40, 8.7, 8.20, 8.43, 8.45, 8.55, 9.0, 9.26, 10.10, 10.35, 11к25, 11.45, 11к58 a.m., 12.15, 12.25, 12к45, 12s50, 12о55, 1о3, 1к9 1.15, 1.25 2.7 2.18, 2.40, 3.0, 3.20, 3.55, 4.5, 4.35, 4.37, 4.45, 5.5, 5.10, 5о20, 5.25, 5к30, 5о38, 5.40, 5о58, 6.9, 6.17, 6.18, 6.35, 6.45, 7.14, 7к8, 7.32, 7.53, 8.15, 9.0, 9.15, 9.50, 10.0, 10.50, 11.0 p.m.	7.0, 7.40, 8.0, 10.0, 10.15, 10.30 a.m., 12.0 noon, 12.50, 2.45, 2.50, 3.44, 4.25, 6.10, 6.25, 6.30, 7.30, 7.42, 8.20, 8.36, 9.30, 10.0, 10.25, 10.30 p.m.
WEST BROMWICH, WEDNESBURY and BILSTON (G.W.)	5.30, 6.30, 7к37, 7.40, 8.20, 8к33, 8к43, 8.45, 9.26, 10.10, 10к35, 11к25, 11к58 a.m., 12к15, 12к30, 12s45, 12к50, 12о55, 1.15, 2.7, 2к40, 3.0, 4.5, 4к37, 4.45, 5.10, 5к30, 5к38, 5.40, 5.55, 6к17, 6.18, 6к41, 6.45, 7.14, 7к32, 7.50, 8.15, 9к15, 10.0, 10к50, 11.5 p.m.	7.0, 7к40, 10к0, 10.30 a.m., 12.50, 2.45, 3к44, 6.10, 6к30, 7.42, 8к36, 9.30, 10к20, 10.25 p.m.
DUDLEY (via Great Bridge)	7.37, 8.43, 10.35 a.m., 12.15, 12к50, 12о55, 2.40, 4.37, 5к30, 5о38, 6.17, 6о59, 7.32, 9.15, 10.50 p.m.	7.40, 10.0 a.m., 3.44, 6.30, 8.36, 10.0 p.m.
WORCESTER, MALVERN, HEREFORD & SOUTH WALES	8.0, 9†10, 10.30 a.m., 1.0, 3.50, 5.0, 5†45, 7†10, 8.20 p.m.	8к0 a.m., 12.0 noon, 5.10, 7†30 p.m.

For Notes see page 495.   Continued on page 495.

GREAT WESTERN RAILWAY.
Emergency Passenger Train Service from Birmingham (Snow Hill)

These Services are liable to alteration or cancellation at short notice.   For details see Company's Time Tables and Notices.

TO	WEEK-DAYS.	SUNDAYS.
SMETHWICK JUNCTION, STOURBRIDGE JUNCTION and KIDDERMINSTER	5.40, 6.15, 6.45, 7м17, 8.0, 8.7, 8.55, 10.30, 11.45 a.m., 12sмq15, 12sм18, 12м25, 12sq40, 1т0, 1См3, 1sмq3, 1sм9, 1.25, 2.18, 3.20, 3.50, 3.55, 4.35, 5q0, 5м5, 5о20, 5.25, 5q45, 5о47, 5о5м58, 6.9, 6о1мq23, 6м35, 7.10, 7к28, 7м53, 8.20, 9.0, 9.50, 11м0 p.m.	8.0, 10.15 a.m., 12.0 noon, 2.50, 4.25, 5.10, 6м25, 7.30, 8.20, 10м30 p.m.
BORDESLEY, SMALL HEATH, TYSELEY & ACOCKS GREEN	5.20, 6.22, 6*50, 7.4, 7.18, 7*32, 7.39, 8.0, 8.32, 8с35, 8с45, 9.6, 11.5, 11.45 a.m., 12.10, 12b47, 12.55, 1s10, 1.20, 2.5, 3.10, 4.20, 4s35, 4о40, 4оy53, 5о10, 5оy20, 5g20, 5о5о55, 5nа45, 5оm47, 6b3, 6.12, 6.45, 7.20, 7о40, 8.20, 9.40, 10.40, 10е50, 11.5 p.m.	9.0, 9е5, 10.28 a.m., 12.25, 12е40, 12р45, 3.35, 3е40, 5.25, 6.0, 7е10, 8.40, 9е45, 9.50 p.m.

A—Banbury only.	F—Via Cheltenham Spa and Gloucester (not to Worcester, Malvern or Hereford).	a—Tyseley only.
B—Smethwick Junction only.		b—Acocks Green only.
C—Not to Reading.	Q—Not to Smethwick Junction.	c—Not to Tyseley or Acocks Green.
D—Wednesbury only.	R—Restaurant or Buffet Car Train, and in some cases for a portion of the journey only.	e—Not to Acocks Green.
E—Not West Bromwich.		g—West Bromwich only.
G—Saturdays excepted.		m—Not to Olton.
H—Not to Bilston.	S—Saturdays only.	
J—To Worcester and Malvern only.	T—Does not call at Smethwick Junction on Saturdays.	n—Shrewsbury only.
K—Not to Knowle and Dorridge		p—Not to Bordesley.
L—Leamington Spa only.	X—Restaurant Car to Banbury.	
M—Not to Kidderminster.		
N—Not to Portsmouth.		
		t—Saturdays only and not to West Bromwich.
		u—Small Heath and Acocks Green only.
		v—To Bristol only.
		x—To Knowle and Dorridge only.
		y—To Bordesley only.
		†—Via Oxford and Didcot.
		‡—Via Oswestry.
		*—Small Heath & Tyseley only.

STATE OF EMERGENCY

During the Second World War the Great Western Railway introduced an austerity train service for its passengers. Adversities, coupled with the much bantered cliché 'Is your journey really necessary?', the blackout, bombing, and delays (due to railway centres being under constant attack by enemy aircraft), brought times of chaos to stretch the resources of even the best disciplined railwayman. In retrospect, the railway companies throughout the length and breadth of the country played a vital part in bringing final victory to fruition. In these extracts from the 1945 emergency timetable some of the Paddington services from Birmingham Snow Hill are listed as conveying Restaurant and Buffet Car facilities, in some cases for a portion of the journey only. At the outbreak of war in 1939, all restaurant car services were suspended but a limited meals service was restarted in 1945 on certain GWR trains, with several new restaurant cars being constructed to mark the event. The first class was upholstered in blue leather tub-seating, whilst the third class was finished in green tip-up style seats. The Christmas menu on these trains was a real luxury for 1945 ration-bound Britain. There was turkey with all the festive trimmings — along with roast pheasant as the chef's speciality!

(D. A. C. Harrison collection)

LET'S GET AWAY FROM IT ALL

Post-war holiday crowds on the booking hall concourse and platform number 12 about 1947. This was still a period of austerity and little or no petrol was available for private motoring, so everybody travelled by train. Certainly between the years 1945-59 passenger traffic increased enormously. The locomotive in the top photograph, looking unkempt and woe-begone, is 'Princess Augusta', one of the many 'Star' class 4-6-0's built earlier this century. For many years Tyseley was its home depot. One can only hope that all the passengers in the picture managed to board the train. If no further accommodation was available, a relief train was usually never far behind. Plans were announced in 1947 to improve traffic and passenger facilities at Birmingham Snow Hill. The number of main line tracks was to be increased by transforming two of the bay roads into through routes. The booking hall was to have been expanded with escalators installed to replace the stairs leading to the platforms.

(Birmingham Evening Despatch/Mrs D. Tipping collection)

The north end of Snow Hill station in 1948 just six months after the Great Western Railway lost its identity. An 'Aberdare' class 2-6-0 freight engine (number 2651) ambles through one of the centre roads with a north-bound goods, years after it should have been scrapped. This class of locomotive dates back to the days of William Dean and was originally built in 1899. A total of 81 were constructed. During the Second World War locomotives with a reasonable amount of life left in them were given a general overhaul and returned to traffic, hence the last 'Aberdare' survived until 1949. Photographed on the 5th June 1948.

(Patrick Garland)

Faithful old plodder — R.O.D. 2-8-0 number 3016 — pauses briefly on the down middle road in June 1953 with a mixed freight train. 3016, bearing its home shed plate number 84B Oxley (Wolverhampton), was built by the North British Locomotive Company, Glasgow, as works number 22123 in April 1919. A fair number of these locomotives were constructed for wartime military freight services to an original 1911 design of the Chief Mechanical Engineer, Great Central Railway, J. G. Robinson. One could never describe the R.O.D.'s as fast freight engines, more 'methodical plodders'. None the less, the locomotives proved very reliable in service at home and overseas in two world wars. Quite a few of them survived to be taken into service with British Railways in 1948. 3016, in fact, survived until October 1956. It was customary for Swindon to adapt the R.O.D.'s for Great Western use, with modified boiler mountings, the standard safety valve bonnet, plus other ancillary items. Incidentally, R.O.D. stood for Railway Operating Division.

(Real Photographs)

How many Midlanders remember the British Industries Fair? This industrial 'Shop Window' staged at Castle Bromwich was the forerunner of today's National Exhibition Centre. For the 1949 occasion Snow Hill station was decorated with flags, bunting, and the B.I.F. symbol of two gear wheels in mesh. This brought a little light relief to the booking hall concourse, but equally interesting is the collection of motor vehicles, all now valuable exhibits.

(Birmingham Gazette/Mrs D. Tipping collection)

''How about a nice cup of tea, Sir?'' — served from this stylish new refreshment trolley which was introduced by the Western Region of British Railways for use at Snow Hill station in connection with the British Industries Fair. Drinks, along with other light refreshments, could be served to passengers at the carriage window — a service which proved extremely popular for many years after its inception. This particular refreshment trolley has now been preserved at the Dean Forest Railway Preservation Centre at Norchard, near Lydney, Gloucestershire.

(Birmingham Post and Mail)

The telegraph office, pictured on the 7th November 1948, when Mr N. Richardson was in charge. At that time he had served the railway for 45 years. This office was literally the nerve centre of Snow Hill station, with the all-important task of sending and receiving messages relating to the running of trains and special consignments. The teleprinter machines which were seldom idle seem somewhat antiquated in comparison with the micro-chip technology of the computerised 1980's.

(Birmingham Gazette/
Mrs D. Tipping collection)

The ticket office of the main booking hall was always a hive of activity, especially at holiday periods. Snow Hill booking offices housed somewhere in the region of one and a half million tickets — mostly stored in the Great Charles Street booking office — but if the odd destination was called for, a Regina ticket printing machine was at hand to print specially requested issues. This machine was certainly the most advanced of its type when installed in 1912.

(Mrs D. Tipping collection)

ONE HUNDRED NOT OUT!

The Birmingham - Wolverhampton Centenary special at Victoria Basin, near Wolverhampton. This train of auto-trailers, hauled by a Collett-designed 0-4-2 tank locomotive, was organised by the Midland Area of the Stephenson Locomotive Society. The Mayor of Wolverhampton, Alderman L. J. Wooldridge, stands on the running plate of number 1438 to welcome the complement of SLS members. The train ran on Saturday 13th November 1954, which was a significant day in the life of driver Bob Wall. It was his last day in the service of the railways and Bob was chosen to work the special as a token of his long service and devotion to duty over many years.

(Birmingham Post and Mail)

Last day of duty — 'Bulldog' 4-4-0 number 3454 'Skylark' entering Snow Hill from the Hockley direction in readiness to haul an SLS special to Swindon on Sunday 17th June 1951. The 'Bulldog' class, as it was generally known, began life in 1899 under the auspices of William Dean, Chief Mechanical Engineer of the Great Western Railway at that time. A further batch was constructed under the Churchward regime up to the year 1910. The 'Bulldogs' were noted fliers in the hands of a good crew, giving many years service during both world wars. A gradual withdrawal of the class commenced in the Thirties, 'Skylark' being the sole survivor before withdrawal in 1951.

(Real Photographs)

STEPHENSON LOCOMOTIVE SOCIETY SPECIALS — VINTAGE MOTIVE POWER STYLE

Another vintage 4-4-0? — not quite. 'Dukedog' number 9000 simmers gently in platform number 7 before taking yet another popular SLS trip to Swindon Works at 10.30am on Sunday 14th June 1953. The term 'Dukedog' is a combination of the frames of withdrawn 'Bulldog' locomotives and 'Duke' class locomotive boilers and fireboxes married to form one complete engine. C. B. Collett designed the class in 1938 for use principally on light lines and cross country routes. Many of these sturdy machines could be seen west of Shrewsbury on the former Cambrian line to Barmouth and Aberystwyth.

(D. A. C. Harrison collection)

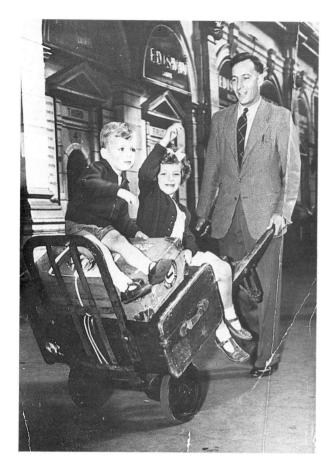

ALL DRESSED UP — WITH SOMEWHERE TO GO

Harold Jones with children Cheryll, aged 5½, and Christopher, 3½, pictured on the booking hall concourse during the summer of 1955. Mrs Stella Jones recalls that it was a beautiful sunny day for the start of the family holiday at Cliftonville. Father utilises a porter's barrow to wheel luggage along with the two youngsters, all eager to board that holiday express. Mrs Jones added that by the time the family reached their destination the children's white socks were not quite so shining white — one drawback of the steam era.

(Mrs Stella Jones)

Gateway to the sea. Prospective holidaymakers queue outside the advance booking office which was situated within the main booking hall itself. In the 1950's and '60's it was essential to book in advance and hold a seat regulation ticket for holiday trains, to eliminate overcrowding. Once all the formalities were dealt with the ticket could take happy holidaymakers to another world. The West of England, the South Coast and North Wales proved extremely popular around this period.

(Birmingham Post and Mail)

RAIL STRIKE — MAY 1955

Rail strike bulletin — during the mid-summer period of 1955 a National rail strike began and during the crisis Snow Hill managed to carry on a skeleton service from the limited amount of trains offered. Even the chalked notices are worthy of merit, for the almost copper-plate script must have provided a dedicated railwayman with a labour of love. The strike was over pay and better conditions and proved once and for all that the railway workers of Great Britain did a vital job in communications. Their grievances were rewarded with a substantial increase in wages and fairer duty sharing.

STRIKEBOUND SUNDAY

Platform number 7 misses the holiday bustle as 4083 Abbotsbury Castle pulls into an almost deserted station on 30th May 1955. Note the mid-fifties fashions worn by the men — where were all the ladies on this sunny afternoon?

(both Birmingham Post and Mail)

LMS-built 4-6-2 'Coronation' class Pacific number 46237 'City of Bristol' pauses alongside the steps leading down onto platform number 7 before departing with the 2.35pm ex-Wolverhampton (Low Level) to Paddington express. 46237 was, in fact, on coal consumption trials when this picture was taken on the 26th April 1955. The results were compared with similar findings from the GWR-built 'King' class 4-6-0 locomotives. Speculation was rife at this time that 'Kings' were a far better, more economical engine. Although both machines were rated almost equal in tractive effort, after collation of the relevant information it was found there was very little difference in overall efficiency between the two locos.

(F. W. Shuttleworth)

An ex-LMS 4-6-2 Pacific, one of the famous 'Princess Royal' class designed by Sir William Stanier in 1933, number 46207 'Princess Arthur of Connaught', runs into Snow Hill with the 2.33pm Wolverhampton-Paddington express in February 1956. This engine was one of several loaned to the Western Region during this period in the mid-fifties when all the 'King' class locomotives were temporarily withdrawn due to fractures being discovered in the front bogie frame. Note the additional support frame on the smokebox door which allowed the Western Region practice of express engines carrying reporting numbers. Also in this historic photograph is the GWR-installed running-in board — BIRMINGHAM — which remained in its original form at Snow Hill for many years.

(Real Photographs)

DAY OUT FOR A DEAN GOODS

The Stephenson Locomotive Society organised many special trains that commenced their journeys to the by-ways of our railway system from Birmingham Snow Hill. This particular special ran on Saturday 28th May 1955, and toured lines in the West Midlands area, including the sleepy once-independent Cleobury Mortimer and Ditton Priors Light Railway. Dean goods locomotive number 2516, now preserved at the Great Western Museum, Swindon, receives youthful admiration before departing from bay platform number 3. The letters OSW on the front of the valance plate denoted that the locomotive's home base was Oswestry, in Shropshire.

(Birmingham Sunday Mercury)

BACK IN SERVICE

Back in service after spending twenty-five years in the original York Railway Museum, record breaking ex-GWR 4-4-0 3440 'City of Truro' propels its train through platform number 6 to run eventually into the opposite side of Snow Hill at platform number 7, in readiness to haul a Stephenson Locomotive Society special train to Swindon on Sunday 1st May 1957. This was the first major rail trip by this locomotive from the Birmingham area since its return to the main line. 'City of Truro' gained fame after its alleged speed of 102.3 miles per hour on 9th May 1904 whilst hauling an Ocean Mails express from Plymouth to Paddington. During its brief turn of duty from 1957 to 1961 3440 would be seen on the Didcot, Newbury and Southampton service when not engaged on special trains. In 1962, after the second withdrawal from traffic, 'City of Truro' was placed in the GWR Museum at Swindon. Then, in July 1984, she was removed and transported by rail to Bridgnorth and the Severn Valley Railway for renovation to full working order as part of the 150th anniversary of the Great Western Railway.

(R. C. Stallard)

DIESELISATION FIFTIES STYLE

Foretaste of the future — AEC-built diesel railcars on experimental trials in the West Midlands area in August 1953. These revolutionary diesel multiple units were the forerunners of the modern cross-country sets that were to grace Snow Hill station some five years later. In this scene, the unit has just run in from Solihull before proceeding on to Stourbridge junction. The information obtained and evaluated proved vital for the diagramming of diesel train services for the future benefit of the travelling public.

(Real Photographs)

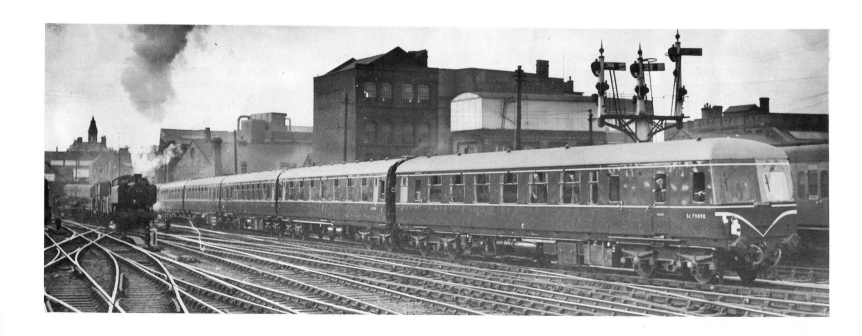

(*Opposite, below*) Diesel debut — in the mid-1950's the Western Region of British Railways introduced lightweight diesel multiple units on various cross-country lines where the running of a through train hauled by steam was impracticable. It was not the first time diesels appeared on long distance services. In 1934 the GWR began a diesel railcar experiment between Snow Hill and Cardiff via the North Warwickshire line, which has already featured in this book. Fresh from the workshops — a brand new six-coach diesel multiple unit enters Snow Hill station on 1st August 1956. The cross-country trains were an immediate success when introduced, being clean, spacious and comfortable, and soon became popular with the travelling public. A freight train struggles through one of the centre roads hauled by one of the post-war Hawksworth-designed pannier tanks, built at Swindon works in 1949. Note the double-scissors crossover trackwork which was a feature of the station.

(Birmingham Post and Mail)

MAIN LINE DIESEL POWER

Class extinct — Swindon-built 'Warship' class number D824 'Highflyer' stands at the head of a Paddington-Wolverhampton express in number 6 platform. The 'Warships' were introduced on the Western Region in the late 'Fifties with D824 commissioned on the 27th July 1960, but lasted in service just twelve years before withdrawal on 3rd December 1972! Diesels somehow do not have the life built into them as did the steam locomotives.

(Real Photographs)

The successor to the 'King' class was the class '4' (later class 52) 2,700 horse power diesel hydraulic locomotive, number D1000 'Western Enterprise' being the first example. This was the first of its type to be built at Swindon and was powered by two German Maybach power-plants. These were certainly the most revolutionary diesel locomotives to be built in this country. Sadly the machines had a short hard-working life of only fifteen years. Five of them, however, are preserved, with two examples at Bridgnorth on the Severn Valley Railway. Special gala days are operated using the Type 52's from time to time. When first built 'Western Enterprise' was painted in an experimental desert sand livery and is seen on a Paddington-Birmingham-Wolverhampton express in platform number 6 on the 11th August 1962.

(B. J. R. Yates)

PRAIRIES ON PARADE

The fresh sunny railway station — that was Snow Hill. In this tranquil scene taken in 1957 2-6-2 'prairie' tank number 4173 shunts empty stock in readiness to return it to Tyseley for servicing and cleaning. During this period, the standard coaching stock livery was carmine and cream, which was quite pleasing to the eye if kept smart. The Empire fruit and confectionery stall on platform number 7 has some choice item to attract the gaze of two passengers, whilst two young trainspotters admire the turnout of 4173.

(R. S. Carpenter)

CAMBRIAN COAST EXPRESS

Of the many express passenger trains that called at Birmingham Snow Hill none had such romantic aura as did the 'Cambrian Coast Express' — mainly because of its lengthy journey. London Paddington to Pwllheli was 303 miles! The 'Cambrian' departed from the capital at 11.10am, calling at Leamington Spa, Birmingham (departure time 1.25pm), Wolverhampton and

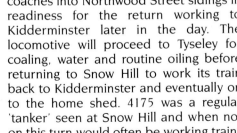

Summer tranquillity, a lull in the busy summer traffic. Ex-GWR 'prairie' 2-6-2 tank number 4175 propels its train of suburban coaches into Northwood Street sidings in readiness for the return working to Kidderminster later in the day. The locomotive will proceed to Tyseley for coaling, water and routine oiling before returning to Snow Hill to work its train back to Kidderminster and eventually on to the home shed. 4175 was a regular 'tanker' seen at Snow Hill and when not on this turn would often be working trains from Bewdley to Wooferton Junction, via Tenbury Wells.

(Michael Hale)

Shrewsbury, where the main line express locomotive was changed for a 'Manor' class 4-6-0, which would take the main train through to Aberystwyth. The 'Manors' were lightweight express engines beloved by the shed staff at Aberystwyth, who kept their paintwork and motion immaculate, especially for the 'Cambrian'. At Machynlleth the train divided. The main portion proceeded to Aberystwyth whilst the remaining part diverged onto the coast line at Dovey Junction, hauled in the late 1950's by an outside-framed 4-4-0 'Dukedog', but replaced in later steam years by one of the many standard locomotive classes. Pwllheli, the far terminus, was reached about ten past seven in the evening after calling at every station and halt en-route. Journey time from London, eight hours! Full restaurant car facilities to Aberystwyth from London were available. Lunch in 1959 — 12/-6d. (62½p), or 15/-(75p), depending on the menu chosen. The photograph above left, taken by W. A. Handscomb in 1958, depicts 'Castle' class 4-6-0 number 5044 'Earl of Dunraven', its single chimney blustering that 'anxious-to-depart' sound, so familiar to any Great Western Railway locomotive about to leave Snow Hill with the northbound 'Cambrian'. The right hand study, taken by John H. Cox in 1959, shows the southbound train minus headboard at platform number 7, hauled by 'King' class 4-6-0 number 6001 'King Edward VII'.

PACKED LUNCHEON AVAILABLE

Autumn sunshine on platform number 7 — afternoon shafts of sunlight illuminate a new packed meals kiosk which was introduced by the Western Region in October 1959. Passengers awaiting the London express could also enjoy a cup of tea before entraining. The destination indicator was a standard item of equipment that was in use at many Western main-line stations to illustrate the arrival of the next train at the appropriate platform. It was merely a matter of slotting the relevant destination board into the central post for each train. The staff and passengers little realised when this photograph was taken that as a main-line station Snow Hill had less than eight years to live!

(Birmingham Post and Mail)

1960-1967   TOWARDS PARTIAL CLOSURE

Death warrant — in the form of a notice of impending closure and withdrawal of main line and some local rail services on the Snow Hill-Wolverhampton line. Due to the electrification of the Euston-Birmingham New Street-Wolverhampton High Level line all express services were transferred to this route on and from Monday 6th March 1967. However, permission was refused to withdraw the local train service from Snow Hill to Wolverhampton Low Level, including all intermediate stations. Although drastically reduced the service lingered on unadvertised until March 1972.
(Charles Aston)

DICK RILEY REMEMBERS

The well-known railway photographer, Dick Riley, spent a couple of days at Birmingham Snow Hill in March 1960. By this time the peak amount of rail traffic passing through the station was at its height. Not only ex-Great Western locomotives were seen on the variety of trains.

An ex-LMS 2-8-0, number 48402, rumbled through (right) with a load of steel scrap from the south bound for Round Oak Steelworks. These locomotives were designed by Sir William Stanier, Chief Mechanical Engineer of the LMS in 1935. Many saw service at home and overseas during World War Two and examples survived until the official end of steam on British Rail in 1968.

6001 'King Edward VII' leaves platform number 6 bound for Wolverhampton (Low Level) with the 1.10pm ex-Paddington on 21st March 1960.

It was during the 1950's-60's, the period when steam still reigned supreme, that R. C. Riley — Dick to his friends — became a household name in the railway press, recording many scenes with his camera, in particular around the Western Region. He also contributed to the recording of railway history in the form of several magazine articles in addition to photographic albums. Two items from the monthly Trains Illustrated spring to mind — 'The Cornish China Clay Traffic' and 'Home With The Milk', both giving detailed accounts of rail working thirty years ago. In March 1960, whilst journeying back from the Stephenson Locomotive Society's 'Last Train' on the former Shropshire and Montgomeryshire Railway, the writer first met up with Dick, as he did on several subsequent occasions over the next twenty-five years, the last being at Paddington where the subject of photographs for this book was discussed. He sent sixteen pictures of which four have been chosen to illustrate the northern approaches to Snow Hill.

6005 'King George II' enters Snow Hill with the 3.33pm ex-Wolverhampton-Paddington express on the 22nd.

Looking towards Paddington with 6005 entering Snow Hill with the same train on the previous day, whilst 4942 'Maindy Hall' labours towards the Black Country with a heavy freight train. A diesel multiple unit waits in platform number 6 — many local services were worked by these three or six car sets.

REQUEST GRANTED

'King' class locomotive number 6002, 'King William IV', as displayed in bay platform number 4 on 8th September 1962. The 'Kings' were all to be withdrawn at the end of September 1962 and as a gesture of goodwill the Western Region displayed 6002 at Snow Hill to mark the end of 35 years of main line service. Bryan Yates of Handsworth Wood, Birmingham, was disappointed on arrival at the station to take a photograph. The locomotive had been awkwardly positioned and it was virtually impossible to focus all the locomotive in the viewfinder. Also the roof canopy put 6002 very much in the shade, but let Bryan tell the full story in his own words . . . . .

"During the week 3rd to 8th September 1962, to commemorate the withdrawal after 35 years' service of the most powerful express passenger locomotive on the Great Western Railway, namely the 'Kings', one of these fine engines, No. 6002 'King William IV', was put on public display beautifully cleaned and polished. Since this was probably the last opportunity I would have to photograph this engine on active service, I arrived at Snow Hill station on the Monday to find the engine pushed up against the buffer stops in the bay alongside platform 6 under the canopy, in a hopeless position for photography, flanked on the opposite side by a rake of coaches. This, together with the people milling around on the platform, made it virtually impossible to take a photograph, and in desperation I had a chat with the driver to see if the engine could be moved back into the daylight to enable me to take a photograph. He was very sympathetic and said he would see what could be done and disappeared down the platform in the direction of the signal box. Some fifteen minutes later he reappeared, accompanied by the signalman, the traffic controller and none less than the Station Master himself. After introductions I explained the position, and following a small deliberation, the Station Master said that as the locomotive was on display for the public to view, he saw no reason why it should not be moved — a simple enough statement in itself, but the traffic manager said this could only be done when the single car diesel multiple unit, arriving at that time on the same line as the locomotive, had offloaded its passengers, adding that it would then have to be moved clear of the platform end in order to clear the signal interlocking sections. The adjoining line would also have to be protected to prevent any train drawing in alongside. The diesel duly arrived and unloaded its passengers. A somewhat taken aback and highly amused motor man was ordered to drive his diesel to the end of the platform clear of the point interlocking bars. The signal box then put all the signals, points, etc in order and finally the traffic manager came along to say that at last the engine could be moved backwards into the daylight to be photographed some one and a half hours after I made my original request. This was done and my photographs duly taken, and everyone, including the driver, seemed well satisfied. The fact that all these people had put themselves out to provide me with this opportunity of taking these now historic photographs was, to me, just another example of the kind, understanding and helpful attitude of all the staff at Snow Hill station; a characteristic of the old Great Western which never died, and indeed was always obvious to all who used the station right up to its closure on 6th March 1967."

A KING'S FAREWELL!

Locomotive 6028 'King George VI' pulls away from platform number 7 with the 10.am express to London Paddington on the 6th September 1962. This was the last week in the life of the 'Kings' as these superb, and without doubt, fine locomotives were all to be officially withdrawn on and from Monday 10th September 1962. British Rail ran a commemorative rail tour from Wolverhampton (Low Level) and Birmingham (Snow Hill) to Swindon on Sunday the 9th September, utilising locomotive 6000 'King George V' for a comparatively modest fare of £1.2/-(£1.10p) return.

(Birmingham Post and Mail)

STRANGERS IN TOWN!

'First day's outing!' Ex-L.N.E.R. 4-6-2 A3 pacific number 4472 'Flying Scotsman', now based at Steamtown Museum, Carnforth, Lancashire, at Birmingham (Snow Hill) on Saturday the 20th April 1963, with the Festiniog Railway Society Annual General Meeting special train, which was run from Paddington to Porthmadog as an opportunity for members and friends to visit the Festiniog and travel behind locomotives less familiar to the old GWR main line. On this occasion over 5,000 people crowded into Snow Hill station. All the platform ticket machines ran out and it was a case then of collecting the 3d admission charge by hand. In spite of the pouring rain 4472 was given a rousing welcome and the writer recalls boarding the train with some difficulty due to the dense crowds, but it was certainly a day out to remember. This was the first public appearance of 4472 since her purchase for private preservation in the autumn of 1962.

(B. J. R. Yates)

Southern Region-rebuilt Bulleid Pacific 4-6-2 number 34028 'Eddystone' enters Snow Hill via the northern approaches with one of the many football excursions run on Saturday the 27th April 1963 from Southampton. An FA Cup semi-final was being played at Villa Park between Southampton and Manchester United and Snow Hill station was invaded by Bulleid Pacifics. Examples of this famous class of steam locomotive, both the air-smoothed casing and the rebuilt version designed in 1956 at BR Workshops in Eastleigh, were to be seen hauling excursion trains conveying fans to this important sporting event. There were, in fact, twelve West Country Pacifics 'up for the Cup'. Here is the full list of numbers and names, supplied by Mr A. Trend of Wednesbury, who was an eye-witness at Birmingham Snow Hill that morning. 34009 'Lyme Regis', 34028 'Eddystone', 34039 'Boscastle', 34040 'Crewkerne', 34042 'Dorchester', 34045 'Ottery St. Mary', 34046 'Braunton', 34050 'Royal Observer Corps', 34052 'Lord Dowding', 34088 '213 Squadron', 34094 'Mortehoe', 34098 'Templecombe'.

(A. Trend)

NEW BRIDGES FOR OLD

In the 1960's a new pre-stressed concrete overbridge was installed at the northern end of Snow Hill as part of a road reconstruction programme in the city. Partial demolition of the canopies was included in this mammoth rebuilding operation. A good deal of planning was needed, with major operations taking place on a Sunday when traffic was minimal.

The two photographs, now part of railway history, were taken after the new bridge had been installed. The famous double scissors crossovers were also removed at this time as these had become redundant — the remains of the connections are clearly seen in the photographs, taken on the 10th April 1964. The top picture illustrates a 9F 2-10-0 built in 1955, No. 92025, fitted with Franco-Crosti boiler.

Ten of these British Railways-built locomotives were so fitted as an experiment — all were subsequently rebuilt with orthodox boilers. Number 92025 is seen here hauling an iron-ore train from Banbury. The lower picture shows another 9F, No. 92001, ambling through the middle road from the Hockley direction with a mixed freight for the south.

As the photographer commented "a casual snap contains so much railway history — at the time, one never realises what one is taking".

(Christopher Bladon)

Youthful admirers stand at platform number 6 on the 18th April 1964 as 2-6-2 tank number 4555 stands at the head of a northbound pick-up freight train. By this time 4555 had passed from British Rail ownership into the hands of two Birmingham businessmen who realised a boyhood ambition to have a steam locomotive of their very own.

This picture shows 4555 on the return working with a heavier local freight — as one of its owners commented at the time "*being flogged to death no doubt*". However, this diminutive 'tanker' did some very useful work in the Birmingham area before departing to work on the Dart Valley Railway in Devon.

(both D. Legg)

END OF
THE LINE

F. W. Hawksworth-designed 'County' class 4-6-0 number 1011 'County of Chester' sits beneath the smoke trough at the end of platform number 12 with a Stratford-upon-Avon semi-fast train in September 1964. 1011 had been in store for some time at the BR steam depot at Tyseley. To ensure all was well, 'County of Chester' made a number of 'running-in' turns around the West Midlands before final cleaning to an immaculate condition in readiness to haul an SLS special train to Swindon. (C. Aston)

'County of Chester' stands sedately in platform number 2 at the head of the return SLS special train from Swindon on Sunday 20th September 1964. Compared with the previous picture 1011 looks good for another twenty years' service, having been checked and cleaned thoroughly. It is difficult to believe that within one week of this trip 1011 would make her last journey to the place of her birth — Swindon — for scrapping.

(D. Legg)

JUST VISITING

EX-LNER A4 Pacific 4-6-2 number 7 — British Rail numbering 60007 — 'Sir Nigel Gresley' roars through Birmingham Snow Hill, its chime whistle giving that resounding melody that was very much the characteristic of an A4 locomotive. To all the railway enthusiasts gathered on the ends of platforms 6 and 8, this must have been a stirring sight. 'Sir Nigel Gresley' was making its last official trip for British Rail on Sunday 24th October 1965, with a specially-chartered train from the north of England. It was rare for an express train to run non-stop through the centre road of Snow Hill and on this rare 'one-off' occasion many of the railway and station staff paused from their duties to stare in almost disbelief at this 'streamliner' from another world. 'Sir Nigel Gresley' is now based at Steamtown Museum, Carnforth, Cumbria.   (Birmingham Post and Mail)

DOOMED GIANT

"Pullman train for Wolverhampton . . . . now standing at platform 5", the speaker announcement would blurt out. This all-luxury train, affectionately known as the 'Blue Pullman' by its many passengers, was certainly the forerunner of the modern day Inter City 125. It was on 12th September 1960 that this revolutionary train was introduced by the Western Region of British Railways. First and second class accommodation was provided, with meals served at each seat. Without a doubt the last word in luxury rail travel for Midlanders. The Blue Pullman was designed and built for BR by the Metropolitan-Cammell Carriage and Wagon Company Limited. Two 1,000 bhp diesel engines, coupled with electric generators and eight traction motors, working in concert, gave a top speed of 90 mph. A thousand gallon fuel capacity was provided, each eight car train weighing 364 tons. Livery for this train was very pleasing. A colour scheme of Nanking blue, relieved by a broad white band, extended the length and width of the windowed section on each of the cars. The Pullman Company crest was carried on the end of each power car and within the white band of each vehicle. A surcharge of 7/6d. (37½p) was made on the normal first and second class fares. On occasions the complete train could be hired for charter use at weekends. If it was out of commission due to a breakdown, or for servicing, a secondary Pullman train was kept as a standby. This consisted of the older style carriages, with their individual armchair comfort, inlaid panels and gilded brasswork. The railway staff at Snow Hill dubbed them the Wells Fargo coaches but when in use a certain sumptuous grandeur pervaded Snow Hill — memories of a long-forgotten era of luxury rail travel.

(Birmingham Post and Mail)

INTO THE RAILWAY HISTORY BOOKS!

7029 'Clun Castle' storms up Hatton Bank with the 'Zulu' en-route from London Paddington to Birkenhead Woodside via Birmingham Snow Hill on Saturday 4th March 1967. This was the second of two special trains to Birkenhead that day. On the following day it was the turn of the Midland Area of the Stephenson Locomotive Society to pay their last respects. 7029 hauled the first train — an ex-LMS 'Black Five' followed with the second. It befell the duty of 7029 to haul the very last train from Birkenhead back to Birmingham — developing problems with a valve spindle midway through the journey. On arrival at Snow Hill, a tumultuous welcome greeted 'Clun Castle'. Hundreds of people turned out to welcome the special and bid 'Dear Old Snow Hill' a tearful goodbye. A shriek of the whistle, a hiss of escaping steam and 7029, with her now empty coaches, headed into the tunnel, the last steam-hauled train to leave the station.

(R. J. Blenkinsop)

SWAN SONG

Farewell, Snow Hill. 1924-built 4079 'Pendennis Castle' about to depart from platform number 6 with the northbound 'Birkenhead Flyer' on Saturday 4th March 1967, being the first of the two trains that day. This particular 'Castle' led a spectacular life and charmed existence towards the end of its career on British Rail. In 1925 'Pendennis' became involved in the Locomotive Exchanges between the main line companies. After many years of top-link working 4079 was eventually withdrawn for storage at Swindon running sheds. In 1963 the locomotive returned to service for odd duties in the Bristol area. The 9th May 1964 was the 60th anniversary of 'City of Truro's' record-breaking run with the Ocean Mails Special. 4079 hauled a commemorative train to Plymouth from Paddington. All went well on the outward journey and the packed special arrived two minutes ahead of time! On the return 96 mph was reached at Westbury when the firebars collapsed and the locomotive was taken out of service. It was fitting, many thought that day, that 'Pendennis' had gone out with a bang. It was not to be forever, however, for Mr M. F. Higson stepped in and bought 4079, including in the deal an overhaul at Swindon. The locomotive was sold eventually to Bill McAlpine who kept the 4-6-0 at Market Overton but major boiler repairs were eventually carried out at the Steamtown Museum, Carnforth. The locomotive remained there until purchased by the Hammersley Iron Company of Western Australia, where she now hauls specials on a private railway. 4079's last passenger run in the United Kingdom was in May 1977, after which she was shipped to Australia from Avonmouth docks.

(Steve Underhill)

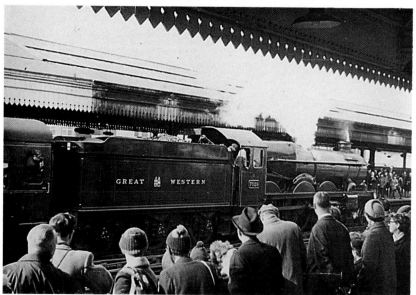

This photograph is from the author's collection, showing 7029 'Clun Castle' at Birmingham Snow Hill on Saturday 4th March 1967, with the second of the specials from London Paddington to Birkenhead.

A unique souvenir handbill specially printed as a limited edition by the late Roger Wilson, who travelled on the last of the SLS special trains on Sunday 5th March 1967. All the various letters and characters were discovered in an old box at a Gloucestershire printers a few weeks prior to the rail tour.

This photograph shows 4079 'Pendennis Castle' at platform number 7 later on the Saturday evening with the return 'Birkenhead Flyer' en route to Paddington.
(Eric Thompson)

Fellowship of Nostalgic Ferro-Equinologists

GENUINE
FERRO-EQUINOLOGICAL
EXCURSION
TRAIN
Fare £2!
COVERED CARRIAGES

SUNDAY
5 MARCH 1967

DEP 9-20 Prompt

TO

BIRKENHEAD

& BACK

OVER THE LINES OF THE

Great Western Railway

FROM THE

Snow Hill Station

DRAWN BY THE LOCOMOTIVE ENGINE

THE "CLUN CASTLE"

(UPON Mr. COLLETT'S IMPROVED PRINCIPLES)

The Whole Trip accomplished

WITHOUT HORSES !

R.Wilson, 'Steam' Printer, Cheltenham

BIRD'S EYE VIEW

Birmingham's vast concrete jungle sprawls as far as the eye can see as this unique aerial photograph reveals. The narrow confined complex of Moor Street station can be discerned as can the entrance to Snow Hill tunnel to the right of this station. The tunnel curves slightly to the right on a rising gradient of 1 in 45 for a distance of 596 yards before Snow Hill station is reached, to the centre right of the photograph. The main line to Wolverhampton left Snow Hill through a shorter tunnel to reach Hockley, with its comprehensive goods depot. This can just be seen in the upper right-centre as a dominant triangular shaped structure. The districts of Handsworth, Smethwick, Oldbury and West Bromwich are lurking in the industrial haze of the Black Country, to the north-west of Birmingham. On the left is New Street station with its twelve platforms partly visible.

(Birmingham Post and Mail)

Wrought iron splendour — no expense was spared when the second rebuilding of Snow Hill station commenced in 1906, even to the extent of ensuring that the side passenger entrance from Snow Hill thoroughfare was decorated to herald a warm welcome onto the main booking hall concourse. As with the main entrance gates, the GWR could be read from either side. After the station was demolished this item of Snow Hill memorabilia was saved by the author. The wrought ironwork was restored to its former glory of red oxide finished in gold leaf and now resides in the reception area of Arthur Young, the Chartered Accountants — approximately fifteen feet from the original position it occupied until 1969.   (Birmingham Post and Mail)

SAVED BY THE AUTHOR

The magnificent wrought-iron gates that led into the booking hall concourse were temporarily locked after the main line closure of March 1967 and not unlocked again until the concourse was prepared for use as a car park. The main booking office was abandoned in favour of a new entrance in Livery Street and the pay train system of issuing tickets. The clock still ticked on methodically for several weeks after the closure but sadly stopped due to the lack of staff to wind it! Note the initials GWR on the centre of the gates. The letters were fashioned with such skill and artistry that the scroll-patterned script could be read from either side of the gates. The Great Western Railway was forever like that, for once one entered its hallowed domain the reminder that one was to travel on the finest railway in the kingdom was never far away. After demolition of the main station complex in 1977 these superb gates were rescued by the author and are now at the Birmingham Railway Museum.

(Charles Aston)

COMMUTERS CLUB

The regular passengers who used the remaining single unit railcar service from Snow Hill to Wolverhampton Low Level hurry down platform number 4 on Friday the 3rd March 1972. This was the last morning 'rush hour' that Snow Hill witnessed, for on the Saturday it was to be the enthusiasts and nostalgia seekers who would turn out to bury the corpse with dignity. The single unit railcar usually carried the same regular passengers each day but in what was suspected to be a deliberate attempt to curtail this service there was little or no advertising of the fact that trains still ran to Wolverhampton from Birmingham Snow Hill. The community spirit was very much to the fore on this service, especially during the winter months when the ladies would bring flasks of coffee and soup along to add a little cheer on bleak mornings.

(Birmingham Post and Mail)

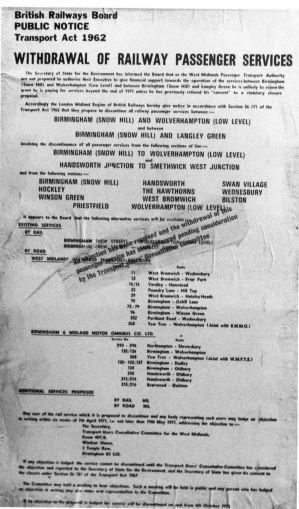

FINAL CLOSURE NOTICE

Illustrated above is the closure notice that was posted in 1971 to spell out British Rail's intention to finally 'kill off' Snow Hill once and for all. As expected, objections were placed with the West Midlands Transport Users Consultative Committee but these found no favour. Thus, the last timetabled service departed early in 1972 leaving behind a decaying hole in the heart of Birmingham.

(Michael Hale)

A rather compressed picture of Snow Hill station viewed from the top of the thoroughfare that gave the station its name. This telephoto shot, taken in 1976, shows the steep incline on which the 1906-1912 station reconstruction took place. In order to overcome problems incidental with the site — lateral expansion was virtually impossible — the new station was constructed on three levels with long platforms extending in a northerly direction.

The fencing that adorned the area around the parcels yard has now found a new lease of life in Broad Street, Birmingham. It protects the bridge above the canal that leads to Gas Street Basin, forming a useful but decorative barrier against the prospects of falling about fifteen feet into the water!

(Birmingham Post and Mail)

DELIVERIES COMPLETED

The parcels office two years after it was abandoned when Snow Hill closed its doors to main-line traffic. In this 1969 shot piles of old paperwork litter the floor, the office furniture is scattered around in disarray and a telephone stands silent and neglected on some clerk's vacant, deserted desk. One of the few members of staff remaining at the station looks somewhat forlorn in the doorway as he sifts through the debris in the hope of finding some treasure.

(Birmingham Post and Mail)

PLATFORM OF MEMORIES

The view along platform number 7. In the distance are the steps leading up to the main entrance area. Gone are the speaker announcements, the famous clock, the station staff and even more sad, the gleaming Great Western locomotives. In their place broken glass and pools of water cover the paving stones that once resounded to the feet of many thousands of travellers in peace and war. The canopies that covered the platform extensions have been cut down, leaving a hoarding of tattered posters in the foreground, serving as a reminder of Snow Hill's happier days, when to step on to one of the sun-lit platforms one felt the holiday had well and truly begun. The next whistle to blow on this platform would be for the demolition men's teabreak — nothing would prevent that.

(Birmingham Post and Mail)

AFTER CAREFUL CONSIDERATION

On departure of the last train service the station lingered on for some six or seven years, being used as a car park. In 1977 British Rail found that it would be possible to demolish the train shed with the scrap metal credits balancing the cost of demolition. At this time the planners were having thoughts about making the shed a listed building and various ideas were canvassed. A meeting took place between British Rail and the planners, at which the responsibilities of maintaining the structure were mentioned. Apart from the car parking there was no income available for maintenance, and the engineers concerned had the perpetual worry that glass could fall onto people below. No serious viable use for a listed building could be proposed and it was agreed that demolition could proceed. The general supervision of the work was carried out by the Divisional Civil Engineer, Mr E. R. Newens, through Mr R. J. Herd (Assistant Divisional Civil Engineer Works), and Mr D. A. Hyde (Buildings & Services Assistant). This decision made all the difference to the future use of the site. It was as if difficulties of demolition were holding back developers, but once it was gone, the BR Property Board was able to negotiate with interested parties.

RELICS REMOVED!

Before the main demolition work commenced the main contractors, L. E. Jones of London, made concessions to various parties in allowing items of historic and practical interest to be removed — right down to literally the kitchen sink! Items such as the barriers from the Great Charles Street Booking Hall were to find a new home on the Severn Valley Railway. Much of the woodwork was ripped out and burned by the contractors. Some of the fumed Austrian oak panelling was saved, as were the red rouge marble counter tops from each of the refreshment rooms. Doors, poster boards, old desks, even the Station Master's door lock, complete with brass door knobs stamped GWR, survived. Almost all the imitation carrara-wear and brickwork was crushed into rubble to be used as hardcore for new road works or to fill in a long abandoned canal. Bits and pieces of stonework were carried off by souvenir hunters — no doubt in use now as doorstops or paperweights!

(both Geoffrey Petch)

1969-1970, 1977-1978   DEMOLITION

''we of the older generation will never forget''

FUNERAL PYRE

Smoke rises once again in Snow Hill station, only this time it is from the blazing bonfires of roof timbers, fed by the demolition workers. In this dramatic picture taken on the 9th March 1977 many of the platform buildings have been reduced to rubble in readiness for the task of dropping the heavy steelwork down to platform level for cutting into furnace-length commodities. It is difficult to imagine now the showplace — the pride of the old Great Western Railway — brought to this ignominious state. In a matter of a few months the whole complex was laid to waste. Only the remains of the platforms indicate the station's former existence.

(Birmingham Post and Mail)

DOOMED ARCHWAY

A demolition workman pauses to witness the final demise of the semi-eliptical arched entrance that once played host to millions of rail passengers. This ornate portal was specially constructed circa 1912 to give easy access to Snow Hill station from Colmore Row. In this sad view, taken on the 20th January 1970, much of the former hotel building and booking hall lies in ruins, with sizeable stone cornices dotted around the former concourse. A number of the more ornate pieces of stonework were sold off to collectors to become decorative shapes in some suburban garden whilst the remainder would end up as rubble on some new roadway or fill in an abandoned canal. This was a tragic end for one of the most attractive station interiors in this country.

(Birmingham Post and Mail)

TOTAL DEVASTATION

A panoramic view of the platforms at Snow Hill looking towards Paddington after the main demolition work was completed in 1978. Only a small portion of the brickwork remains to be removed in the south-east corner, but much work remains to be done to bring the area up to the required standard as a car park. The trackbed will be filled in up to platform level and the remaining debris cleared away. After removal of the steelwork that supported the booking hall, the tunnel portals were exposed to the open air for the first time in over 65 years. The remains of the former water crane swing at a drunken angle — its life blood taken away — serving as a final memorial to the once proud Snow Hill.

EDWARDIAN EDIFICE

(Right) The battered facade of Snow Hill ticket-issuing windows in 1976. It was during the period 1969-70 that the overall roof spanning the booking hall concourse was removed, along with the former hotel building. The demolition contractors had little thought for the significance of the carrara-ware marble pilasters and porticos, for as each portion of the steelwork toppled to the ground it struck the facade, delving great gouges out of each cornice as it fell. After the debris had been cleared the former concourse remained open to the sky, elements and the vandal. The remains of the former booking hall reverted to a car park until demolition of the main station buildings in 1977-78.

(both Birmingham Post and Mail)

BUILDING FOR THE FUTURE — A NEW USE FOR A FAMOUS PLATFORM

Up, up and away, the paving slabs from platform number 6 are removed for a new lease of life at Toddington, Broadway and Winchcombe stations on the now preserved Gloucestershire/Warwickshire Railway. In the background the new Sun Alliance Insurance building takes shape. Around sixty feet of the original tunnel portals were demolished to the Colmore Row pavement line before the main construction work began. Allowance has been made for rail access through the tunnel once more, giving a better penetration into the city centre from the Dorridge and Shirley direction. The West Midland Passenger Transport Executive are funding the initial construction work with a £250,000 grant to bring the line back into Snow Hill from Moor Street station, situated on the far side of the city. New platforms will be built at both Snow Hill and Moor Street. Part of the existing booking office at the latter will be retained, whilst the remaining portion will eventually be demolished. The tunnel is 596 yards long.

(Mick Perry)

READY FOR THE NEXT GENERATION?

Hockley tunnels looking towards Snow Hill, pictured on the evening of 15th June 1984. The track bed is littered with debris from the modern throw-away society — hopefully to be replaced by newly-laid ballasted track. Note the peeling white-painted sighting panel on the brickwork to the left of the larger arch — a reminder of when the semaphore mechanical signalling system was in common use on our railways. This panel gave a clear background to the driver in order for him to ascertain the exact position of the signal arm. One day new local train services will use these tunnels with perhaps the odd steam-hauled special from the south visiting Bewdley on the Severn Valley Railway. A pipe dream — but a glorious possibility.

(Derek Harrison)

ARMISTICE DAY — 1922

Four years after the cessation of hostilities on the 11th November 1918 the fallen are remembered in a service on platform number 7. The proceedings here are officiated by the Lay Bishop of Birmingham, Hamilton Baines, along with other civic dignitaries. Frederick Taylor, to the right of the picture, was Assistant Station Master at Snow Hill until 1921, when he was promoted to full Station Master. In the background is the Great Western Railway War Memorial — these illuminated address style documents were especially produced and framed in English oak for presentation to many stations on the GWR system. The names of all former Great Western Railway employees who made the supreme sacrifice during 'The Great War for Civilisation 1914-1918' were listed.

(Nesta Taylor collection)

RECORD BREAKING MAN

Sir Malcolm Campbell chats with Snow Hill Station Master, F. A. Taylor, on the main booking hall concourse during the late 'Twenties. Sir Malcolm was visiting Birmingham in connection with a series of oil promotions for his world-famous 'Bluebird' land speed car. He also visited the Blue Bird toffee works at Hunnington, Halesowen, to endorse his name on tins of confectionery. In those lively years immediately following the First World War, speed was the talk on everyone's lips. Note the interesting motor car, along with the immaculately-liveried chauffeur — a reminder of days long since past.

(Nesta Taylor collection)

THE STRONG ARM OF THE LAW!

Snow Hill's GWR policemen pose with members of the Birmingham Watch Committee in front of a timetable display board on platform number 12, shortly after the close of the First World War. On the right of the board is a poster proclaiming 'GREAT WESTERN RAILWAY, THROUGH COMMUNICATION, GREAT WESTERN AND THE SOUTH EASTERN & CHATHAM RAILWAY', thus pin-pointing the period to within the few years before most independent railways in the United Kingdom were 'Grouped' into four main rail companies. Ann Wyatt, who joined the British Transport Police in 1955, owns the photograph. She can still remember the day she was interviewed as a prospective police candidate at Snow Hill station. This was in a small office situated at the top of a stone spiral staircase in the police headquarters attached to the station in Great Charles Street. After training, plus study at the Epsom Police College, Ann was promoted into the plain clothes division taking up duties in an office at Snow Hill, situated in the subway that ran between platforms 5 and 7 near to the railwaymen's canteen. A permanent smell of cooking, especially cabbage, permeated the police office! Plain clothes officers stationed at Snow Hill during the mid-fifties included DC Albert Hester, DC Stan Jones, Det. Sgt. 'Sailor' Hayes, Det. Sgt. Harold 'Pigpen' Fleetwood and Det. Sgt. Norman Smith. The policewomen, PW Dorothy Doughty, PW Lorna Lewis and PW Parsons, as Ann Wyatt was known in those days, were allotted to such cases as ticket frauds, fare evasion, missing luggage and parcels. PW Doris Banks was the uniformed constable. Inspector Sully, who was in charge of this office, commuted daily from Shrewsbury. He was a police officer of the old school who always expected to see a uniformed police officer on duty on platform 7 as he arrived at 08.55 on the Birkenhead-Paddington businessman's express. The Divisional Police Headquarters for the Western Region was situated on the fifth floor of the old Great Western Hotel. The Police Chief was Mr Galloway and his Assistant Superintendent Harold Wickens, along with Chief Inspector Charles Steed. "All very tall and impressive" remembers Ann. "Two chauffeurs were at the disposal of these senior police officers, with immaculately polished 1953 Austin A135 Princess Limousines. Two spaces were alloted for these cars on the main booking hall concourse". A uniformed policewoman was on duty supervising traffic and car parking on the Snow Hill concourse. Chauffeur-driven cars frequently met businessmen, civic dignitaries and very often celebrities. The pigeons nesting in the roof girders of the concourse could be a nuisance and were avoided at all costs for 'dropping-spotted' uniforms were marked forever! Travelling Ticket Inspectors were employed to investigate ticket and fare offences. Service personnel from HM Forces were up to many 'dodges', including transferring tickets which were specially coded for use by male and female travellers. Ann recalls the main service camps visited on ticket fraud enquiries — RAF Shawbury, RAF Cosford, Royal Army Ordnance Corps Kineton Depot and Budbrooke Barracks, home depot of the Royal Warwickshire Regiment. "The hot summer of 1959 was particularly memorable. The Left Luggage Office at Snow Hill complained of a terrible smell and a large number of bluebottle flies! There had been a hunt for a missing child in the Midlands for several weeks — it was generally feared the child had been murdered — so with trepidation two police officers went to investigate. The large American tourist's canvas holdall was opened to reveal a huge joint of venison and the general opinion was that it had been obtained illegally! The smell was awful." Runaway children also turned up at Snow Hill, usually seeking refuge in the comfortable rest lounges and refreshment rooms. If a child was alone for any lengthy period, the attendant would contact the transport police. Quite a few adventurous youngsters would only get as far as Snow Hill in their attempt to gain independence. A final comment. The requests for old Snow Hill photographs can very often evoke a whole string of memorable events surrounding them. Sadly, no information exists as to the identity of any members of the GWR policemen or the civilians in this photograph.

(Ann Wyatt collection)

ROYAL PROGRESS

The Prince of Wales, later King Edward VIII, is welcomed by the Lord Lieutenant of Warwickshire and the Chief Constable on platform number 5 after alighting from a Paddington express on the 16th October 1931. The Prince was in Birmingham to visit the BBC studios in Broad Street and to deliver a message over the air to Home Service listeners. He was a popular figure in Birmingham, making several visits (sometimes by air to the local Castle Bromwich aerodrome) to the British Industries Fair situated nearby. The Prince expressed tremendous interest in this notable industrial event, as indeed he did in the British Trade Fair held at the Bingley Hall. An important function attended by His Royal Highness was a reunion of the Grenadier Guards Old Comrades at the New Inns, Handsworth, Birmingham, where the large function room was renamed the Prince's Suite, in honour of the occasion. If an overnight stay was planned, this was usually arranged through the Earl and Countess of Dudley, whose home, Himley Hall, was made available for such occasions. The Prince of Wales would frequently travel back to London from Snow Hill in a specially reserved first-class compartment, arranged by the Station Master. The Duke of Windsor was very much a man of the people.

(Nesta Taylor collection)

AN AFTERNOON VISIT

The 1st December 1931. The Duke and Duchess of York arrived at Birmingham Snow Hill at 1.10pm to be greeted by the Lord Lieutenant of Warwickshire, Lord Leigh, accompanied by Lady Leigh. Also present were the Lord Mayor and Lady Mayoress, Alderman and Mrs J. B. Burman. Lady Helen Graham was in attendance as lady-in-waiting and Commander H. G. Campbell as the Duke's equerry. The Chief Constable, Sir Charles Rafter, was at hand to ensure all went well for the Royal visit. The Duchess recognised Frederick A. Taylor, the Snow Hill Station Master, from a previous visit to Birmingham in November 1929 and shook him warmly by the hand. After the formalities, the royal party proceeded to the Council House for lunch before commencing a three hour visit to the Birmingham Cattle Show at Bingley Hall. Fashion historians will note the Duchess of York dressed in a long grey coat with a deep fur collar. A tight-fitting wedgewood blue hat, with matching accessories, crowns this delightful scene at Snow Hill.

(Nesta Taylor collection)

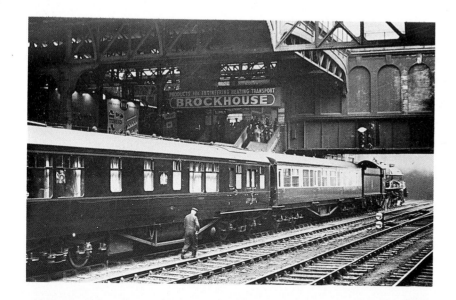

Home in time for supper! H.M. Queen Elizabeth, the Queen Mother, descends the steps to platform number 7 on the 2nd May 1957 for her return to London by the 'up' 'Inter-City' express hauled by 6005 'King George II'. A special Great Western-built saloon, number 9006, along with a brake composite, is attached to the front of this regular service train. 9006 was one of two special saloons used frequently by the Queen Mother in the 1950's and '60's. Both vehicles are now on exhibition at the National Railway Museum, York.

(Michael Mensing)

HRH THE PRINCESS ELIZABETH — THROUGH THE CARRIAGE WINDOW

Saturday the 9th June 1951 saw Birmingham bedecked with flags, bunting and all the panoply relevant to a right royal visit. Princess Elizabeth was greeted at Birmingham's New Street station by the Lord Mayor, Alderman Ralph Cyril Yates, and other civic dignitaries, for a six hour visit to the city. A motor drive to Ladywood followed, passing the Children's Hospital where patients and members of staff gave the Princess a tremendous welcome. A visit to the Bingley Hall, where a Home Fair was in progress, was also made. After a Civic Centre welcome, Princess Elizabeth inspected a selection of veteran cars, including a 1900 Daimler originally owned by her great grandfather, King Edward VII. A rally run to Coventry was waved off by the Princess who then proceeded to Victoria Square to unveil a recast bronze statue of her famous ancestor. A Civic Luncheon at the Council House ensued before a motorcade proceeded to Villa Park, where Princess Elizabeth was guest of honour at a gymnastic display by Birmingham schoolchildren. What a lovely picture the Princess makes through the carriage window as she leaves Birmingham for the return journey to London, dressed in a dull moss green fitted coat of heavy corded silk. Note the charming hat in the same colour, with a square fluted brim of straw giving an almost Tudor appearance. The je ne sais quoi — a diamond bow brooch at the lapel. Nine months later the world would hail her as Britain's new monarch.

(Birmingham Post and Mail)

IN LATER YEARS — HER MAJESTY QUEEN ELIZABETH II

Almost twelve years later, on Friday 24th May 1963, Her Majesty The Queen walks from the Royal Train along platform number 5 with the Lord Mayor, Alderman Dr Louis Glass. The Duke of Edinburgh follows closely behind with the Lady Mayoress, Mrs Glass. A seven hour visit to the city is about to begin, with the highlight of the day the official opening of the new eight million pound Bull Ring Shopping Centre. The Royal Train, hauled by one of the recently introduced diesel hydraulic locomotives, 'Western Emperor', arrived two minutes early in the capable hands of driver Harry J. Mason and his second man Godfrey Morris, both natives of Birmingham. The royal couple were also greeted by the Lord Lieutenant of Warwickshire, Lord Willoughby de Broke, along with the High Sheriff of Warwickshire, Lieutenant Colonel Arthur Chamberlain. The Queen has chosen a superb outfit of bright primrose yellow and navy — a loose fitting yellow wool coat surmounted by a pill-box hat trimmed with a navy silk bow. A sparkling sapphire and pearl pendant brooch, with a necklace of pearls, completes this cameo of royal events at Birmingham Snow Hill, to remind us all of the many joyous occasions witnessed at this famous station.

(The Birmingham Post)

A LETTER OF THANKS

One of the oldest, and possibly the longest, season ticket holder to use the Great Western Railway, from 1874 to 1939, was Brigadier General Sir Walter R. Ludlow of Lovelace Hill, Solihull. Sir Walter sent a photograph of himself in full ceremonial dress to A. H. Elsden as a token of esteem for all the courtesy shown to him by the GWR over the years. Mr Elsden sent it to the Great Western Railway house magazine who published it with a copy of the letter in November 1939. Here the original hand-written letter is reproduced.

(Mrs D. Tipping collection)

Walter. R. Ludlow
Brig: Gen:
1939.

K.C.B.

From BRIGADIER GENERAL SIR WALTER LUDLOW, LOVELACE HILL, SOLIHULL

TEL. 0029 SOLIHULL.   STATION: WIDNEY MANOR G.W.R.

October 9th 1939

Dear Mr. Elsden

Will you give me the pleasure of accepting the enclosed photograph of an old Season Ticket holder on the G.W.R from 1874 to 1939

I wish to express my thanks to the company for the great courtesy and attention that they have shown to me for so many years.

With kind regards and best wishes Believe me to remain

Yours sincerely

Walter. R. Ludlow

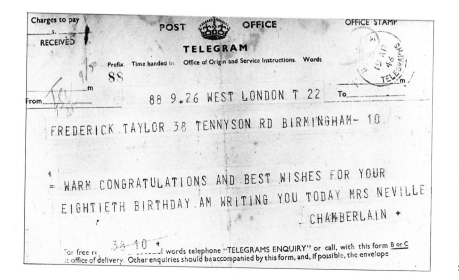

STATIONMASTER REMEMBERED

Frederick Taylor held the post of Station Master at Birmingham Snow Hill from 1921 until he retired in 1932. The characteristic portrait picture was taken especially for Mr Taylor's 80th birthday in 1946 by the Birmingham Weekly Post. Anne Chamberlain, the widow of Prime Minister Neville, sent birthday greetings in the form of a telegram with a promise to write personally. Mrs Chamberlain, true to her word, did so. The original telegram, along with the hand-written letter, is reproduced here. These valuable items have been kindly loaned by Nesta Taylor, F. A. Taylor's daughter. This Station Master was remembered with great affection by the many travelling members of the public and notable personalities, especially the Duke of Windsor, who referred to Mr Taylor on numerous occasions as "a damned good sort".

(Nesta Taylor collection)

ARTHUR HAMMOND ELSDEN

Arthur Hammond Elsden, pictured left at the north end of Snow Hill just before he retired. Note the original style 'pill box' station master's hat. On ceremonial occasions it was always silk top hat and tails, of course.

(Birmingham Evening Despatch/Mrs
(D. Tipping collection)

A safe journey and a happy retirement. Arthur Hammond Elsden bids farewell to Dr John Fisher, then the Archbishop of Canterbury, as he is about to board the 6.10pm to London Paddington. This was the last duty performed by A. H. Elsden as Station Master of Birmingham Snow Hill. Mr Elsden retired in July 1950, and handed over to Mr C. Swancutt.

A. H. Elsden, out of uniform, pictured in his office on platform number 7 where all the day's work was planned and VIPs entertained before entraining.

(Birmingham Post/Mrs D. Tipping collection)

FULL REGALIA

Mr C. Swancutt, dressed in the full Station Master's regalia, poses adjacent to a 1957 timetable at Snow Hill. Mr Swancutt had just been appointed to Cardiff (General) as Station Master, a post which he held for several years before returning to Birmingham yet again, this time as Station Master of Birmingham New Street — as far as it is known the only person to hold the post at the two Birmingham stations. Sadly Mr Swancutt died in office before he could see the reconstructed New Street station completed.

(Birmingham Post and Mail)

HAPPY REUNION

There were four Station Masters on Snow Hill station for a short period during a happy reunion in the early 'Fifties. Left to right:- Mr F. Taylor, 1921-1932; Mr T. Blea, 1932-1936; Mr A. H. Elsden, 1936-1950 and Mr C. Swancutt, 1950-1958. From time to time these meetings were arranged to revive old memories and the opportunity for previous station masters to come along and see dear old Snow Hill once again.

(Birmingham Post and Mail/Mrs D. Tipping collection)

TRAIN SPOTTING TRIO

These youthful train enthusiasts look somewhat pensive as they wait on platform number 5 in the early morning sunshine on the 5th August 1962. All three are obviously anticipating a rare locomotive appearance. Perhaps a seldom-seen 'Castle' or 'County' class, spotted the day before, hopefully might put in another appearance. Judging from the picture the scene is strangely tranquil for a Bank Holiday — the diesel multiple unit is about to depart for all stations to Stratford-on-Avon from platform number 7. Wymans bookstall is lacking custom at the moment but no doubt the books and magazines are laid out in impeccable order.

(Birmingham Post and Mail)

PIGEON FANCIER!

Sunshine and shadow on platform number 5 as passenger shunter Maldwyn Edwards feeds the pigeons in between duties on the 29th March 1967. Contrasting photographs could be taken at Snow Hill if the sun was in the right place. This usually occurred between 12 noon and 2pm. Snow Hill was a difficult location to secure the perfect railway photograph but with care and a little know-how the photographer could capture the atmosphere on film as well as any artist. By the time this picture was taken, Snow Hill ceased to function as a main line station and only a small number of local services ran into the almost deserted platforms. In 1968 the tunnel at the southern end of the station was closed completely, leaving the track at the northern end to survive until 1972.

(Birmingham Post and Mail)

MEMORIES OF THE MINI SKIRT

Christine Doherty sits on her suitcase at the end of the former platform number 7 waiting for a non-existent train. The permanent way has ceased to be permanent and as the weeds begin to sprout Christine checks her watch amid rust and ruination. Cars are parked where once stood the finest steam locomotives in the world. At the time of this photograph — December 1972 — the structure of Snow Hill station was deteriorating rapidly.

The platform buildings became a haven for dropouts and thieves but even in its dying years the mystique remained — to walk down the steps again onto the dust-covered platforms could still evoke memories.

(Birmingham Post and Mail)

POINTS OF VIEW — FROM THE RAILWAYMEN

Mr R. Wright, Station Foreman, pictured in the main booking hall concourse just before the main line closure in 1967. Mr Wright had a firm fondness for 'dear old Snow Hill' — to him it was the Great Western version of the Crystal Palace.

(Birmingham Post and Mail)

Due for retirement — Frank Jeavons, a top link driver of the prestige Birmingham Pullman diesel train, pictured at Tyseley just two months before finishing a fifty year career on British Railways. It is interesting to note that the maximum rate of pay in 1966 for a top link driver was £16-19/-. (£16.95) for a 42-hour week. However, with overtime of ten or twelve hours this amount could be increased further.

(Birmingham Post and Mail)

GONE WITH REGRET

Three ex-GWR men stand amid the ruins of Snow Hill station. From left to right, Mr David Hoccom, Mr Harold Taylor and Mr Stanley Lawrence, pictured in July 1977 when the final stages of demolition were almost complete. David Hoccom recalled joining the Great Western in 1937 as a booking clerk at Bordesley — *"the old GWR was noted for the quality and loyalty of its staff".* Mr Hoccom served as a Warrant Officer pilot during World War II but gave up a comfortable instructor's job in the services at thirty five shillings (£1/75p) a day with allowances, plus food and keep, to return to the railway. His first pay for a fortnight's work was just £6. *"My wife was reduced to tears",* he remarked. *"Discipline on the GWR was tough — almost frightening",* commented Stanley Lawrence. *"Discipline could also be eccentric — imagine a locomotive depot housing over a hundred engines all belching smoke whilst all around the shed walls were notices saying 'No Smoking'!"* Harold Taylor added, *"Foremen were feared but respected — they were like fathers to you really. If one strayed from the paths of righteousness then a fatherly talk would soon put you back on the right road again".* All three had a fondness for Snow Hill. *"It was like no other station in the country",* Stan Lawrence claimed. *"It is sad to see it all like this, but with modern railway progress it had to go",* he said.

(Birmingham Post and Mail)

PROUD OWNERS AT SNOW HILL 1963

Patrick Garland, with Patrick Whitehouse, pose with their very own steam locomotive at Snow Hill — ex-Great Western Railway 2-6-2 prairie tank number 4555, built at Swindon works in 1924. In 1963 careful negotiations culminated in the purchase of number 4555 for private preservation. Part of the agreement was that the locomotive would be given an overhaul at Swindon before being repainted in rich Brunswick green. The side tanks were then lettered 'Great Western' and the bufferbeams painted red with shaded numbers 4555 inscribed thereon. For a period this privately preserved engine worked special trains around Birmingham and the West Midlands. When not employed on these 4555 was used on local pick-up freight duties and also, on odd occasions, the 5.25pm semi-fast passenger train from Birmingham Snow Hill to Knowle and Dorridge. Commuters descending the steps onto platform number 7 were delighted to see such an immaculate engine at the head of their train — *"A touch of days gone by",* one traveller was heard to remark. Number 4555 even gained unrecorded notoriety on the 24th August 1964 when rostered to assist the Pines Express from Leamington Spa to Birmingham Snow Hill. The diminutive prairie tank was first marshalled next to the train with 'Hall' class 4-6-0 number 6991 'Acton Burnell Hall' acting as pilot. The train set off at

2.40pm, arriving at Snow Hill at 3.08pm — a journey of 24 miles, including the 1 in 100 climb at Hatton bank! A signalman who witnessed the event at Lapworth swears to this day that . . . . *"the train was doing over 70 and gaining time"* . . . . *"The thought of those small driving wheels turning at that speed was a trifle worrying to say the least — especially when the engine is your own!"* remarked Patrick Whitehouse. Number 4555 is now stationed on the Dart Valley Railway in Devon, hauling admiring visitors and holidaymakers on this independent railway between Buckfastleigh and Totnes.

(Birmingham Post and Mail)

THE END OF THE LINE

The end of the line is not far away for Snow Hill, held by many as the epitome of Great Western main line railway stations. This final picture, seen through the lens of a Birmingham Post and Mail photographer on a cold wet January evening in 1972, is just a month or so before the final departure of the local service to Wolverhampton Low Level. The very last train of all was a Pullman Car Special from number 1 platform — Birmingham Snow Hill to Stourbridge Junction, then back into the slick modernity of Birmingham New Street. As far as is known, this was the only train to run between the two stations. There let us leave it to slumber awhile before a new awakening, when sizeable trees and undergrowth will hopefully be swept aside as track, trains and speaker announcements re-appear to give new life and a new era.

(Birmingham Post and Mail)

GONE BUT NOT FORGOTTEN